GOVERNMENT PROCEDURES AND OPERATIONS

E-GOVERNMENT

PERSPECTIVES, CHALLENGES AND OPPORTUNITIES

GOVERNMENT PROCEDURES AND OPERATIONS

Additional books and e-books in this series can be found on Nova's website under the Series tab.

GOVERNMENT PROCEDURES AND OPERATIONS

E-GOVERNMENT

PERSPECTIVES, CHALLENGES AND OPPORTUNITIES

ANIL SIEBEN
EDITOR

Copyright © 2020 by Nova Science Publishers, Inc.

All rights reserved. No part of this book may be reproduced, stored in a retrieval system or transmitted in any form or by any means: electronic, electrostatic, magnetic, tape, mechanical photocopying, recording or otherwise without the written permission of the Publisher.

We have partnered with Copyright Clearance Center to make it easy for you to obtain permissions to reuse content from this publication. Simply navigate to this publication's page on Nova's website and locate the "Get Permission" button below the title description. This button is linked directly to the title's permission page on copyright.com. Alternatively, you can visit copyright.com and search by title, ISBN, or ISSN.

For further questions about using the service on copyright.com, please contact:
Copyright Clearance Center
Phone: +1-(978) 750-8400   Fax: +1-(978) 750-4470   E-mail: info@copyright.com.

NOTICE TO THE READER

The Publisher has taken reasonable care in the preparation of this book, but makes no expressed or implied warranty of any kind and assumes no responsibility for any errors or omissions. No liability is assumed for incidental or consequential damages in connection with or arising out of information contained in this book. The Publisher shall not be liable for any special, consequential, or exemplary damages resulting, in whole or in part, from the readers' use of, or reliance upon, this material. Any parts of this book based on government reports are so indicated and copyright is claimed for those parts to the extent applicable to compilations of such works.

Independent verification should be sought for any data, advice or recommendations contained in this book. In addition, no responsibility is assumed by the Publisher for any injury and/or damage to persons or property arising from any methods, products, instructions, ideas or otherwise contained in this publication.

This publication is designed to provide accurate and authoritative information with regard to the subject matter covered herein. It is sold with the clear understanding that the Publisher is not engaged in rendering legal or any other professional services. If legal or any other expert assistance is required, the services of a competent person should be sought. FROM A DECLARATION OF PARTICIPANTS JOINTLY ADOPTED BY A COMMITTEE OF THE AMERICAN BAR ASSOCIATION AND A COMMITTEE OF PUBLISHERS.

Additional color graphics may be available in the e-book version of this book.

Library of Congress Cataloging-in-Publication Data

Names: Sieben, Anil, editor.
Title: E-government: : perspectives, challenges and opportunities / edited by Anil Sieben.
Other titles: E-government (Nova Science Publishers)
Description: Hauppauge, NY : Nova Science Publishers, 2020. | Series: Government procedures and operations | Includes bibliographical references and index. |
Identifiers: LCCN 2020006797 (print) | LCCN 2020006798 (ebook) | ISBN 9781536175639 (paperback) | ISBN 9781536175646 (adobe pdf)
Subjects: LCSH: Internet in public administration--Case studies. | Political participation--Technological innovations--Case studies.
Classification: LCC JF1525.A8 E2365 2020 (print) | LCC JF1525.A8 (ebook) | DDC 352.3/802854678--dc23
LC record available at https://lccn.loc.gov/2020006797
LC ebook record available at https://lccn.loc.gov/2020006798

Published by Nova Science Publishers, Inc. † New York

CONTENTS

Preface		vii
Chapter 1	E-Government, Yesterday, Today and in the Future *Idongesit Williams*	1
Chapter 2	Enterprise Architectures in the Local E-Government Context: A Systematic Literature Mapping *Daniela Gallegos-Baeza, Ignacio Velásquez, Angélica Caro and Alfonso Rodríguez*	41
Chapter 3	Empirical Evaluation of e-Government Using a Combination of Decision Making Methods *Katerina Kabassi*	67
Chapter 4	Why and How South Korea Became the World's Best E-Government Country: Focusing on the Leadership of President Roh, Moo-Hyun *Choong-Sik Chung*	89

| Chapter 5 | Determinants of Citizens' E-Government Adoption Services in Greece
Anastasia Voutinioti | 137 |

Index 163

PREFACE

E-Government: Perspectives, Challenges and Opportunities begins by addressing an investigation conducted in a current EU project wherein it was made evident that the successful interplay between institutions and technology makes the digitization of government services possible.

The authors present the results of a systematic literature mapping that reviews the adoption level of enterprise architectures in local e-governments. These results will indicate where and how enterprise architectures have been used, which frameworks are used for their definition, and possible challenges and opportunities for their utilization in the local e-government context.

An empirical evaluation that combines two different Multi-criteria decision making techniques, called AHP and TOPSIS, is provided, along with steps that must be taken to apply these theories in comparing e-government sites.

A report is included on Korea's electronic government policies during the Roh Moo-hyun administration. President Roh Moo-hyun was directly engaged as a developer in the e-government development team, designing document management and task management processes with experts. The fact that the president of a country directly participated in the development of the e-government system remains a rare case in the world.

Additionally, citizens' behavior is investigated in conjunction with the role of "Citizen Service Centers" in e-government adoption in Greece, with the goal of contributing to the understanding of the users' motivations.

Chapter 1 - What makes the digitization of either a government service or a portfolio of government services successful? What elements have to be in place to enable the digitization and delivery of government services? In the course of an investigation conducted in a current EU project, it was evident that the successful interplay between institutions, the technology and the government service that makes the digitization of such a service possible. If this interplay does not succeed, then the government service will not be digitized. This feedback was revealed in archival research backed by the theory of institutions as promoted by W.R Scott. The archival research reveals initiatives ranging from the 1800s until today; and how the successful interplay of institutions, government services and technology resulted in the digitization of either individual government services or a portfolio of government services.

Chapter 2 - Nowadays, governments increasingly use Information and Communication Technologies, both for supporting their internal processes and for providing products and services to citizens and the industry. This style of government is known as e-government. An important advantage of e-government is that it provides the potential to improve the efficiency of processes and the scope of governmental services. This is especially fundamental in the context of local governments, or municipalities, as they are relevant participants in the well-being of citizens and in the development of their corresponding communities. This is because municipalities are the governmental entity that is closest to the community and that generates the greatest impact on it. Thus, the incorporation of technology must be consistent with the objectives of municipalities and its efficacy must be constantly assessed by the citizens. To achieve this, being able to visualize the existing alignment between the objectives, services, processes and supporting technology becomes essential. This would allow to more adequately approach, through the support of information technologies, the constant evolution that is confronted in municipal management. A strategy to accomplish the above is the creation of the municipality's Enterprise Architecture. An Enterprise Architecture provides a holistic view of an organization. This allows identifying its motivational components, as well as the processes, services and supporting technology, the relationships of these components and the principles of the organization's design and evolution. In the last years, they have recurrently been proposed as a framework for e-government initiatives and as a means for obtaining standardization, convergence and interoperability. Due to this, the interest to learn what is the adoption level of Enterprise Architectures in municipalities across the world arises. Thus, this chapter focuses on presenting the results of a systematic literature mapping that reviews the adoption level of enterprise architectures in local e-governments. These results will allow to learn where and how have Enterprise Architectures been used, to see what frameworks are used for their definition, and to identify possible challenges and opportunities for their utilization in the local e-government context.

Chapter 3 - The significant investments made by governments around the world in developing e-government capabilities make it essential to evaluate them systemically; if they are to improve the value they generate. One of the critical issues for both researchers and the governments is how to evaluate and assess the value of such projects. Therefore, Kunstelj & Vintar focus on the need for evaluating e-Government and express the need for improved methods of evaluation. As a result, evaluation of e-government implementation has attracted the attention of researchers within the last two decades and some research work in this domain has been conducted evaluating government websites. However, as Sterrenberg points out, past studies that involve evaluating e-government have been somewhat limited, despite the fact that e-government has had an important impact on the way public services have been delivered in recent years. In view of the above and in an effort to present a well-established evaluation experiment of e-Government, the authors present an empirical evaluation that combines two different Multi-Criteria Decision Making Techniques, called AHP and TOPSIS. The paper summarizes and presents the steps that need to be taken for the application of these theories in comparing e-government sites based on criteria that have been collected using the outcome of the literature review of AHP evaluation studies of e-Government. The evaluation experiment compares five sites for e-government in Greece with the participation of 78 real users. Greece was selected as it is a country that tries hard the latter years to improve the way the government services are performed and improve e-government.

Chapter 4 - Today, South Korea is regarded as the world's best country in the field of e-government. In the most recent UN e-Government Survey conducted in 2018, South Korea ranked third after Denmark and Australia. In addition, it was ranked number one in the UN e-Government Survey three times in a row from 2010 to 2014. As such, South Korea is recognized as a global leader in e-government. The e-government systems utilized in Korea today have been implemented and completed in the days of the Roh Moo-hyun administration. On August 14, 2003, the 'Roh Moo-hyun Administration e-Government Vision and Principles' was announced and was followed by the 'e-Government Roadmap.' The e-Government Roadmap was composed of four areas of innovation, 10 agendas, and 31 projects. During the period from 2003 to 2007, a total budget of USD 981 million was invested in e-government implementation. President Roh, Moo-hyun's insights and intentions toward the electronic government were reflected in the e-government projects in Korea and hence Korea's electronic government policies achieved great results during the Roh Moo-hyun government. When President Roh, Moo-hyun took office in 2003, UN e-government ranking of South Korea had remained outside the top 10; it improved to be ranked 5th by the end of his term in 2008 and soon achieved world's top place by 2010. President Roh, Moo-hyun was directly engaged as a developed in the e-Government development team to design document management and task management processes with experts. The fact that the president of a country directly participated in the development and diffusion of the e-Government system remains a rare case in the world. As such, e-Government can be successfully pursued if the president's will and leadership are firmly established. But there is a dilemma here. Eventually, the president is replaced and the new government takes office and thus it is important to ensure the permanence of the e-government policy. In this case, it is necessary to designate a national CIO and institutionalize it, not solely depending on the ability of the president's own leadership. Therefore, the Republic of Korea is still indebted to President Roh, Moo-hyun for the success of the e-government.

Chapter 5 - This research aimed to investigate citizens' behavior and the role of the 'Citizen Service Centers' (CSCs) in e-government adoption in Greece. The ultimate aim was to contribute to the understanding of the user's intention drivers or barriers in the e-government take-up, building a theory, and proposing a validation research framework. It validated the UTAUT2 model in the Greek context, by using a quantitative research approach, focusing on the CSCs that act as intermediaries. The SEM validation of the proposed model revealed that 'performance expectancy', 'trust in the government', 'trust in the Internet', and 'effort expectancy' were vital drivers that positively influenced the users' intentions. The 'habit of going to CSCs' was negatively related to users' intentions. This meant that the way CSCs operate did not help in e-government take-up. At the practical level, the research provided e-government policymakers and web designers with practical recommendations to better plan, design, and implement policies to increase the e-government take-up.

In: E-Government
Editor: Anil Sieben

ISBN: 978-1-53617-563-9
© 2020 Nova Science Publishers, Inc.

Chapter 1

E-GOVERNMENT, YESTERDAY, TODAY AND IN THE FUTURE

Idongesit Williams[*], *PhD*
CMI, Department of Electronic Systems,
Aalborg University, Denmark

ABSTRACT

What makes the digitization of either a government service or a portfolio of government services successful? What elements have to be in place to enable the digitization and delivery of government services? In the course of an investigation conducted in a current EU project, it was evident that the successful interplay between institutions, the technology and the government service that makes the digitization of such a service possible. If this interplay does not succeed, then the government service will not be digitized. This feedback was revealed in archival research backed by the theory of institutions as promoted by W.R Scott. The archival research reveals initiatives ranging from the 1800s until today; and how the successful interplay of institutions, government services and technology resulted in the digitization of either individual government services or a portfolio of government services.

---

[*] Corresponding Author's E-mail: idong@es.aau.dk.

Keywords: institution, e-government, government services, public services, technology, institutional theory

1. INTRODUCTION

This chapter provides an insight on how the interplay between institutions, technology and government services influences e-government service delivery. The insight is based on evidence from both historical and contemporary literature. This provides insight into how the three elements mentioned earlier, jointly enabled e-government service delivery. Hence the bases for the title, "yesterday," "today" (2019) and "the future." The scope of service discussed in this chapter is not about holistic government service delivery by a country. Rather it is about the delivery of single e-government service. Examples include data processing, tax, business registration etc. These services could be either bundled or delivered individually. In the case of a bundled service, it is still considered a 'single service portfolio.'

This chapter is inspired by an interesting observation from a current EU Interreg funded research project. This project is called the Digital Innovations Network. The aim of the project is to facilitate digitization, aimed at promoting a Digital Single Market (DSM) in the Baltic Sea Region (Williams, Falch and Tadayoni 2018). As part of this project, the project partners collaborated toward providing technical and policy solutions that will enable cross-border e-government service delivery. In principle, they are already dealing with the e-government of the future. Nevertheless, one of the findings in the course of solving the problem was that Cross-border e-government services would not be possible if it lacked institutional legitimacy at the national level (Williams, Falch and Tadayoni 2018). Furthermore, cross-border e-government service delivery can only become feasible if the technology enables the government service in question and if there is institutional legitimacy for the adoption of the technology to deliver that service (ibid).

This finding triggered curiosity on whether the interaction of these three elements did influence e-government service delivery over the years. In literature, there is a great deal of research dealing with the influence of institutions on e-government service delivery (see examples (Eom 2012) (Salifu-Siddi and Williams 2016) (Kim , Kim and Lee 2009) (Manoharan and Ingrams 2018). Furthermore, there is also a great deal of research dealing with the impact of technology on e-government service delivery (Kraemer and Dedrick 1997) (Fontain 2001) (Heinze and Hu 2005). However, research dealing with the mutual influence of these three elements towards e-government service delivery is rare. The work of Jane Fontain contains these elements, but their mutual relationship is not the focus of the work (Fontain 2001). Hence, an archival research was launched to find out if these three elements have always, from time immemorial, influenced e-government service delivery and if it will do so in the future. Examples of evidence found over the years in some part of the world are documented in this chapter.

This book is divided into 5 sections. The introduction is followed by an overview section explaining the relationship between institutions and government services. The next section provides a brief overview on how the examples were identified and the criteria for choosing the examples. This is followed by two sections explaining how the interaction between institutions, government services and technologies influenced and will influence e-government service delivery in the past, present and future. The final section provides a discussion on the practical implication of the findings.

2. OVERVIEW OF E-GOVERNMENT, GOVERNMENT SERVICES AND INSTITUTIONS

Although the focus of this chapter is on the three elements, Institutions, Government services and Technology, two of the three elements have always operated together from time immemorial. These elements are institutions and government services. Government services are also known as public services. Government services are services that are of general interest and are provided by government agencies to its classes of citizens (Bauby, Simile and Raimbault 2010). Government services could be delivered electronically, hence e-government or with the aid of technology. Before explaining the relationship between government services and institutions, it is important to define e-government as used in this chapter.

E-government is a concept with varied but related definitions. These definitions are in most cases inspired by the contemporary views on e-government and e-governance initiatives. These views are influenced by the idea that e-government is a phenomenon that emerged in the 1990s (Grönlund and Horan 2005). Examples of such definitions identify e-government either as the use of Information and Communication Technologies (ICT) to facilitate government services (Fang, 2002); or the use of the internet to facilitate government service delivery (Weerakkodya, El-Haddadeh, Sivarajah, Omar, & Molnar, 2019); or the use of web-based applications to facilitate government services. (Lemon, Holden, & Preece, 2003). The challenge is that these views possess delimitations on technologies that can, have or will, in the future, facilitate e-government. The reality is that e-government service delivery actually dates back to the 1800s (West 2004). Obviously, the form of e-government service delivery in those days was primitive and limited in scope. The technologies that enabled e-government in those days, as will be revealed in this chapter, were either Tabulator Technologies, Telecom Technologies, Information Technologies or Communication Technologies. In the future, we are not so sure of what technology will enable the e-government service of that day. Hence, from this perspective it is not wise to rely on some of the limiting contemporary definitions of e-government.

Therefore, based on this premise, the definition for e-government adopted for this chapter is the use of technology by government services (Silock 2001). The use of the word, technology removes the technological limitation and enables the identification of historical e-government initiatives that were ignored. E-government services could either be Government-to-Government (G2G), Government-to-Business (G2B),

Government-to-Citizens (G2C) and Government-to-Employees (G2E) services (Hanna 2010). These services could be either information dissemination (online or otherwise); information exchange (online or otherwise); or transactional services. These services could be either sectoral (vertical) services, horizontal services (citizen or national centric) or digital democracy services (ibid). Digital democracy services includes e-voting etc.

As mentioned earlier in this section, government services and institutions go hand in hand. Without institutions, government services would not exist. In our world today, it is evident that national institutions govern government services' delivery. Nevertheless, what do we mean by an institution in this chapter? Institutions in this chapter, does not refer to organizations but to rules, regulations, norms and schemes (North 1990). In other words, institutions are also referred to as the 'rules of the game' (ibid). Institutions are important because they provide the basis of order for societies, organizations, and communities (Dimaggio and Powell 1983). The basis of order prescribes the acceptable behavior or actions and provides mechanisms towards enforcing the order (Scott 1995). In the absence of the basis of order, chaos is likely. This is why organizations, communities and society, adopt laws, norms, schemas etc. to regulate actions, processes, tasks, portfolios and services within their ecosystems. Based on this premise, one would say that it is the institution that mandates the delivery of government services and in some cases prescribes how the service should be delivered and which office holder or government agency should deliver the service.

Despite these seemingly straight forward explanations of what an institution is and how it works, there is no consensus on the frameworks that describes an institution (see examples (Sott 2001) (North 1990) (Williamsom 2000)). This in part has to do with the fact that there are nuances in institutions in various economic sectors and as viewed from the lens of various academic disciplines. Nevertheless, a framework that works well, and seems to provide an overview of an institution, is the works of R. W. Scott. In his framework, institutions are either regulative, normative or cognitive (Scott 1995). Regulative institutions include rules, laws etc;

normative institutions are norms and values; while cognitive institutions are shared meanings or schemas (ibid) (Silock 2001). The regulative institution constitutes formal rules, while the normative and cognitive institutions are informal rules (Sott 2001). Each institution exists because it is legitimate. For the regulative pillar, the institution is legitimate because it is legally sanctioned; for the normative pillar the institution is legitimate because it prescribes the right thing to do; and for the cognitive pillar, the institution is legitimate because it is either culturally accepted or the conceptually correct thing to do (Sott 2001).

R. W. Scott's framework works well for e-government services. Development agencies such as the World Bank have adopted the R.W. Scott's worldview when discussing institutions in relation to e-government service delivery (World Bank 2016). Institutions that govern e-government services include legal mandates; organizational or cultural norms; or either shared meanings or acceptably culturally acceptable practices imposed upon government agencies as they mimic either other government agencies or organizations in the service delivery process (ibid) (also see example (Savas 1978)). These institutions legitimize the delivery of government services (including e-government services). The attempt to deliver a government service outside the confines of regulative, normative or cognitive institution can be viewed as illegitimate. Hence, in order to legitimize such actions, then an institution has to be introduced via some form of change management process. Therefore, there is an intricate relationship between government services and institutions. So how does this play out with technology?

3. METHODOLOGY

Before proceeding to the finding, it is important to provide a brief summary of how the examples were found. The online search for archival material was via Google Scholar, databases associated with the Aalborg University Library and Google search. The first part of the search was to search for historical books explaining how government agencies used technologies from the start of the industrial age in the late 1700s. The search was performed using custom search parameters on Google scholar. That is where there were leads to materials from databases such as Jstor, Wiley, Proquest search; old newspaper articles in archives; and many 19th century books accessed via Google books. To assist in the process, information from the Computer history Museum, historical websites and other sources of technological timelines were used to guide the search process. Though helpful, in most cases it was not adequate. This was because in some of the materials, there were references in the 19th century literature to what historical figures might have omitted. Hence, there was also a snowball effect in the search for information. The same process was adopted for the custom search of every ten-year interval with keywords derived from the technology, the existing institution (law, norms conventions, acts etc) and government service of which the technology was capable of performing. The findings were for the yesteryears (1800s - 2018), today (2019) and the future (2019 upwards).

There were lots of dead-ends with initiatives which the supporting institution alluded to, but they were difficult to find. Those initiatives are not mentioned. Nevertheless, the lack of evidence of such initiatives do not invalidate the conclusions of the chapter. Furthermore, another delimitation of the investigation was that the initiatives mentioned in this chapter are mostly North American and European. Few initiatives from Asia, South America and not the least Africa, are mentioned as well. This is not to imply that very few initiatives occurred in the latter. Rather, it is because most of the initiatives found in the course of this investigation were from North America and Europe. This does not imply that the relationship between the three elements are only valid on the two continents. In the course of the research, as will be mentioned later in this section, evidence points to the fact that the three elements also hold in other continents as well.

The findings indicate that from the 1800s onwards, these technologies, namely electronic tabulator technologies, computers and telecom networks played independent roles in facilitating government services. The electronic tabulator is the ancestor of the modern computer. Therefore, it is grouped under the computer in this chapter. The telecom networks identified were the Electronic Telegraph, the Telephony (fixed and mobile) and Broadband Internet networks. The optical telegraph would have been mentioned but aside from the technology being used for military purposes, there was no evidence that it supported either a G2B, G2C or G2G service delivery, hence, it was not considered. However, today, these technologies have evolved and converged and but are now playing a synergic role in the facilitation of government services. Hence, the research on the influence of institutions did revolve around these technologies. The findings are presented in the next section.

4. THE THREE ELEMENTS AND E-GOVERNMENT SERVICES YESTERDAY AND TODAY

This section provides an insight into how the interaction between institutions, government services and technology influenced e-government in history and today. This section is divided into two sub-sections. The first two sub-sections provide information into initiatives that occurred in the past. The last two sub sections provide information on initiatives that occurred in the recent past and today. Furthermore, the first sub-section provides some examples of institutions, government services and telecom network technologies. Here, the network technologies discussed with limited examples are centered on the Electric Telegraph, telecom networks and broadband networks. The second sub-section provides some examples of institutions, government services and computers. Here the network technologies discussed with limited examples are centered on the punch card (electric tabulators), 2nd generation computers, 3rd generation computers and personal computers (PC).

4.1. Institutions, Government Services and Telecom Network Technologies Yesterday

4.1.1. Electric Telegraph

The electric telegraph was a telecom network that enabled direct G2G correspondence. As an example, in 1883 the White House, the capitol and government agencies within proximity to one another were interconnected using the telegraph (House.gov 2019). The network also enabled indirect G2B and G2C services in most parts of the world. Here, government agencies utilized the telegraph to disseminate relevant G2B and G2C information to newspapers, who would then retransmit it to businesses and citizens (The Sydney Morning herald 1878) (Blondheim 1994). However, the electric telegraph was not developed for enhancing the delivery of government service, rather, it was developed to facilitate immediate remote correspondence in society.

In its nascent years from the 1830s onwards, a cognitive and normative societal institution emerged as businesses and citizens in the Americas and Europe grew to adopt the technology. Hence, it became a culturally accepted practice to use the telegraph to facilitate long distance communication but also to support organizational activities. The telegraph enabled fast decisions to be made in organizations. However, despite this emerging institution being enabled by the electric telegraph, government agencies were not early adopters of the technology. In the US, before 1838, government agencies were not able to envision how the technology would support its services (See example (House.gov 2019)). In China, the telegraph was initially viewed as a threat to national sovereignty (Knuesel 2017). In France, there was already an extensive optical telegraph network which was utilized for military purposes (Koenig 1944). They did adopt the electric telegraph until after the British government, who were late adopters as well (Clayton 1997). Aside from that, its network effect, which when compared to the postal service, was low; it was also costly (Green 1883) (Lindley 1971) (Hubbard 1883); and the messages transmitted had to be brief (Choudhury 2010). Hence, government agencies could not immediately mimic organizations.

However, over time there was a diffusion of this institutional influence to the governmental agencies. This diffusion was via demonstrations and the usefulness of the technology exhibited by its maturity. An example of the demonstration was seen in the US. In the US, Morse had to make a demonstration on the usefulness of the technology to congressional representatives. This led to congress funding him, in 1844, to demonstrate how two government agencies can be interconnected (Nonnenmacher 2019). A successful connection of the capitol and the Supreme Court raised the interest of the White House and later in 1833 other agencies as mentioned earlier were interconnected. This kind of direct and indirect change management process highlighted the potential network effect for G2G correspondence or information exchange. It also enabled G2C and G2B information dissemination services, because government agencies could broadcast information meant for citizens and businesses simultaneously to newspaper companies who were already connected to the telegraph network (Blondheim 1994). The situation was the same in Europe in the early days of the telegraph (Morse 1914). The adoption pattern varied. In the US and in Europe, in some cases, the government agency had a telegraph room, in other cases, the agency relied on either telegraph offices at train stations or later at post offices.

Nevertheless, as more government agencies adopted the service, a limited normative institution emerged. Therefore, in the facilitation of government functions, such as diplomacy, the use of the telegram was the right thing to do. Nevertheless, the problems surrounding the cost of telegrams was not "really" solved in the US (Lindley 1971). This hampered a greater adoption of the electric telegraph in the US. For example, Indian agents in the US were directed to only use the telegraph for message delivery if the matter was urgent (Smith J. Q., 1877). Europe actually found the solution by introducing regulative institutions that nationalized the telegraph services (Carré 1993) (Williams 2015). Although these regulations were not aimed specifically at reducing the cost of telegrams for the delivery of government services, they benefitted from it too. Furthermore, in order to ensure that telegrams were neither lost in transit nor delayed, regulative institutions were instituted in both continents to ensure that government messages had priority (Wells 1873) (Highton 1852). Hence, governments were growing to understand the usefulness of the technology and therefore developing institutions to enable smooth service delivery.

The influence and usage of the telegraph for e-government services developed in Europe and the US. The need for diplomacy with China and Japan (Knuesel 2017) (Yang 1996) and the need to interconnect their growing colonies led European governments to extend telegraph networks to Africa and Asia (Quevedo 2010) (Boyce 2000). Hence, European governments facilitated the change management process, which extended the existing cognitive institution governing remote communications in the west to other parts of the world. As a result, Morse code, which is a technical regulative institution that emerged from the US and disseminated to Europe by Americans, became a global institution.

Based on the examples provided, it is evident that without the mutual influence of institutions, the technology and the government service, the electric telegraph would not have been adopted to deliver government information dissemination services. Before discussing telephony, it was interesting to note that the extent, in which the electric telegraph was either adopted or influenced by the institution, did depend on how much it influenced the government service. The electric telegraph could only facilitate information delivery and exchange, and even then not as much as the postal service. This limitation led to the electric telegraph being conceptualized as a supplement to the postal service. In most cases it was referred to as "electronic mail" or mail delivered over electricity (Clark 1895), even though it did not supplant the mail system. The telegraph was also in some cases called the "postal lines" (The Sydney Morning herald 1878). Hence, institutions created, were to enable it to function better rather than improve upon its design to better fit or enhance other government services.

4.1.2. Telephony

The second network technology where the mutual influence between technology, institutions and government services was evident was telephony (fixed and mobile). From its invention in 1876, until the early 1990's, fixed line telephony (first analogue and later digital) played a significant role in e-government service delivery. Part of its decline in the 1990s was because of the commercialization of analogue mobile telephony and its evolution into a digital mobile telephony in the 2000s. Telephony was a disruptive innovation to the telegraph because it enabled a more interpersonal experience in remote communications. The interpersonal experience was made possible by the transmission of human voice. Hence, it enabled voice services. Over time, other services such as document exchange via facsimile and best effort video and multimedia services became possible with telephony. However, in the 1870s, it was mostly voice services. Facsimile existed, but it was not a mature technology and not widely used then. It was in the 1980s that it gained commercial traction.

Despite the advantages of early telephony, its adoption was hampered by its initial lack of network effect in society (Hall and Khan 2002). Its network effect emerged at the invention of telephone switches in the 1890s, which led to the expansion of telephone networks. However, despite this upgrade, the telegraph was already legitimized as a cultural accepted means of information exchange in society in the 1870s. As a result, the telephone did not have institutional legitimacy as a means of communication in society. Furthermore, it had no institutional legitimacy as a means of communication of government services. For example, in the UK the postmaster general indicated that "the telephone was not suitable for public telegraphy" (Holcombe 1906). Even in cases where there was curiosity, its usefulness was not evident. This is why the US President Rutherford Hayes who adopted the telephone a year after Bell's patent remarked: *"That's an amazing invention, but who would ever want to use one of them?"* (Elon University 2019). Actually, at this time, he had only Bell to communicate with (Merrill 2019). It was one year later that the US Treasury Department was connected to the White House.

The private sector and early inventors in both Europe and the US drove the expansion of the telephone from the 1860s to the 1900s (Williams 2015) (Engel 2007). In this period, telephony adoption in the US grew from 3000 to 356 000 telephones (Martin 2017), while in the UK by 1899, the National Telephone Company had about 100,000 subscribers (SMG 2019). Although the number of subscribers were low compared to the national population, the network effect of the telephone emerged, helped in no small part by telephone directories. Hence, subscribers, knew those connected and could contact the switchboard to be connected to the other subscriber. This resulted in the telephone gradually emerging as an acceptable means of communication in society. Furthermore, G2G correspondence was enhanced and citizens and business either could contact or be contacted by government agents thereby facilitating G2G and G2C information exchange or advisory services.

However, just as in the case of the telegraph, the role of telephony in facilitating government services was limited to correspondence. This was because; a couple of decades after 1900, telephony could only facilitate information dissemination and diplomacy (Young 1890). Policy makers did not see that much difference between the telegraph and the telephone. They were electric mails (Clark 1895). Hence, in the 1900s, telephony was nationalized in Europe as part of the postal and telegraph services. It could be inferred that without the active expansion of telephony by the pioneers of the technology, it might not have been adopted for the delivery of government services. Therefore, it is evident in this case, just as in that of the telegraph, that the level of compatibility of the technology to the government service was important.

Although the cognitive institution existing in society did support the adoption of the telephone by government agencies, it was not strong enough to trigger an evolution in the technology to support more government services. The telegraph and postal services backed by their respective institutions were in place. However, there is evidence that the cognitive institution did trigger more adoption of telephony by government agencies for G2C correspondence. An example was in the case of the Social Security Administration in the 1980s (US congress 1989). In a hearing before the Special Committee on Aging at the United States Senate, it was stated that aging citizens preferred to call in than pay personal visits to the Social Security agencies for face-to-face meetings (ibid). Hence, the technology and the institution did influence how the government service is delivered, leading the government agency in question to lean towards the technology.

Despite the role played by cognitive institutions in the early days of the telephones, as telephones evolved, government agencies designed rules for how it should be used for correspondence. These rules were aimed, in most cases, at preventing abuse of the telephone and most importantly, to decide the boundaries for which they will be used for service delivery. These rules were necessary to ensure that telephones did not replace the official means of correspondence in G2G, G2B and G2C service delivery. In most cases, the official means of communication, as mandated by law, is via letters sent through the postal service or telegram (see example (CIA.gov 1968)). In countries, such as Denmark where that is no longer the case, the official means of communication is now by digital post. Hence, telephony (both fixed and mobile) did not gain regulative institutional legitimacy as an official means of correspondence.

Based on these examples, it is evident that the extent to which telephony, be it mobile or fixed-line telephony was utilized for the delivery of government services was influenced by the nature of the technology and the governing institutions.

4.1.3. Broadband and Broadband Internet Networks

The third network technology where the interplay between institutions, technology and government services can be seen is with broadband and broadband internet networks. Broadband networks are an evolution of telephony (fixed and mobile) networks with greater throughput and data rates (Patil, Karhe and Aher 2012). The network capacity of broadband networks enables the simultaneous transmission of heavy data packages (multimedia and video) and low data packages such as voice and text. The previous telephone network could only handle voice and text but not simultaneously. Voice calls had priority in the network. Internet networks, on the other hand, implies the global connection of millions of computers using the internet protocol (IP). More on this computer networks is discussed in the next section. As interest in internet services grew in the early 2000s, newer versions of broadband networks, especially that of mobile networks now relied on the internet protocol. Examples include LTE, WiMAX etc. Nevertheless, broadband networks such as fiber optics that did not rely on IP still enabled the transmission of the internet. Broadband enabled quality of service and quality of experience of the internet. Broadband also emerged at a time, when the internet was mature for commercialization and the experience for using technology to facilitate e-government services had grown.

The development of broadband globally is heavily influenced by the need to deliver digital government services to businesses, citizens, and governments (see Sweden as an example (Regeringskansliet 2011)). If one follows the trajectory of the examples provided, it is evident that by the 1970's governments in the west and Asia were on the lookout on technologies that will enable e-government service delivery. This is because of the experiences gathered over the years. The normative institutions existed in the form of ICT policies as will be discussed later when discussing PCs. International institutions were developed to support visions or frameworks for e-government service delivery. The G8 had the global coverage of broadband as an agenda (Rogers and Reardon 1999). Hence, once broadband technologies were introduced, government agencies in Europe and Asia were prepared as described earlier. This evidence can be found in broadband policies drawn by some countries in Europe, most notably, Germany, Scandinavian countries, France etc. (Williams 2015). Hence, national and international institutions were one of the drivers for the clamor for broadband.

Due to experience with technological restrictions that came with telephony, government agencies were interested in influencing the service delivered by the technology. Hence in the broadband strategies, they prescribed the operational parameters of the technology in terms of speed and what it should do. There was political will in Europe and in Japan, and later China to fund the development of these infrastructures. This will enable government agencies to be connected to citizens and businesses as well as with other government agencies. The facilitation of this network effect would then enable government agencies to provide online e-government services to citizens, businesses, employees and governments. Hence, institutions were used to shape the mode of service delivery and the outcome of the service. Furthermore, if there was no need for the service, the technology would not have been influenced and the institution left untouched.

In order to deliver the new government services using broadband, often times there is the need to change or create a law. If not, then it would be illegal to implement the service. For example, in Denmark a new law had to be enacted to make the delivery of some government services digital and mandatory (DIGST 2019).

4.2. Institutions, Government Services and Computers, Yesterday and Today

4.2.1. Punch Cards (Electronic Tabulators)

It is believed that the prospect of information technology as an enabler for government service delivery was revealed first by mechanical calculators and later punch card tabulators (Nonberg 1990). However, the usefulness of punch cards towards enabling government service processes and later delivery was not evident from the onset. The utilization of punch cards for facilitating processes in government service delivery first occurred in 1890. This was the adoption of punch cards for the compilation and tabulation of the 1890 census results in the United States (Census.gov 2018) (Hollerith 1894). Herman Hollerith invented the punch cards used for the census process and eventually rented the system to the US. As narrated by Hollerith, he had to modify the punch cards to fit the task of compilation, and tabulation of census results (Hollerith 1894). Hence, it was the public service, in this case the census service that influenced how Hollerith's version of the punch card would be developed. However, due to the high cost of rent from Hollerith, the US census bureau developed their own punch card machine to aid subsequent census data computation processes. Aside from the US, the punch card was also adopted for the 1911 UK census (Agar 2003) and the 1907 Cuban census (Nonberg 1990).

When Hollerith conceived the punch cards, the technology was widely used by businesses. Hence, there was a cognitive institution or shared meaning on the use of punch cards for automated tabulation in data processing in the 1800s (read (Hollerith 1894)). Hollerith's proposal towards automating the census tabulation process was aimed at mimicking data processing of huge statistical datasets as performed by the private sector. Hence, he was influenced by the cognitive institution governing data processing of that day in order to facilitate efficiency in the delivery of the government service. However, in order to ensure that the technology fits the task, he had to modify the technology to accommodate the unique tasks at the US Census Bureau. Once successful, he designed a regulative institution of rules on how to use the technology to deliver the service efficiently. Hence, with these rules on how to use the machine, the technology would become easy to adopt by uninformed or untrained operators.

Hollerith's initiative was a risk because the US Census Bureau could have rejected it. In this case he was lucky because the Census Bureau had the constitutional latitude to decide how to perform its task and the census officials were aware of the potential of the electric tabulators to make their work easier. Hence, there was no institutional barrier either from society or at the bureau impeding his initiative. The success of Hollerith's machine in the 1890 census led to the adoption of the technology. An aspect of the service that led to the adoption of the technology and institution was the ability of the punch card to rapidly process huge statistical data sets with high accuracy (Hollerith 1894). For subsequent elections, the bureau developed their own replica of Hollerith's machine to facilitate the data processing activities of the census (Census.gov 2018).

The success in the use of the punch card or electronic tabulators for tabulating election results in the US resulted in its adoption for other record keeping processes by US government agencies (Nonberg 1990). It was used for the management of health information and the American Social Security system in the 1930s (ibid). The cognitive institution resulting in this norm that developed over the years as few other US agencies began with the US Census Bureau. It could be said that the punch card was the first electronic device that inspired the journey to e-government service delivery, as we know it today. However, this would not have occurred without the mutual influence between technology, institutions and government services.

4.2.2. 2nd Generation Computers

When the first generation computers were developed in the 1950s, it was only available for the military (Steitz 2006). Although there has been an evolution of different versions of the punch card, the technology magnified the potential for rapid data processing and analysis. The US Census Bureau was interested in the advanced tabulation capacity and data analysis capacity of the 1st generation computers (Census.gov (a), 2018). Hence in 1946, based on the envision census and statistical processes they needed computers for, they provided requirement specifications and financing from the National Bureau of Statistics to the developers of the 1st generation computer (ibid). The outcome was the UNIVAC-1. Hence, the first computer to be made available to the public was inspired by a government service. The UNIVAC-1 became the new tool for data processing both in Europe and in the US, not just for government agencies, but for the military and businesses (Calhoun 1956) (CHM 2019). This implies that the government service shaped the development of said technology.

This process would not have been possible, if there were either cognitive, normative or regulative institutional barriers impeding either the funding process, the production or the use of the technology by the bureau.

Other 2nd generation computers were available but did not gain the same traction as UNIVAC-1 hence it was widely adopted globally. These computers supported processes behind G2G and G2E services at government agencies. These computers could handle statistical computations that could result in the utilization of data to make forecasts and most of them were store-program computers. However, what was important in the facilitation of government service delivery was that its government agents could produce, aggregate, tabulate, retrieve via printing and analyze data for decision-making processes.

The adoption of 2nd generation computers, after the UNIVAC-1 around the world by government agencies was limited. For example, in the US, excluding those computers meant for defense, federal agencies in the US had adopted about 524 computers and wanted more (US congress 1960). In Europe, apart from the foray of IBM, most countries were developing their own version of second-generation computers and government agencies were waiting to adopt the computers (Calhoun 1956). One of the reasons for the limited adoption of these computers was that they were often rented from the manufacturers. The case of the Census Bureau is rare, as they had to find funds to develop theirs. Therefore, agencies that would have adopted computers could not ask for it. On the other hand, there is evidence that regulative institutions were introduced to limit the adoption of computers (US congress 1960). The reason was to safeguard data processing jobs, which were declining as computers were introduced (ibid). These regulative institutions slowed down the adoption of computers, despite the usefulness of the technology and the compatibility of the technology to the data processing services.

4.2.3. *3rd Generation Computers*

In the early 1960s, the evolution of the computer became a major driver to the evolution of e-government services. This time it was not a government agency, but research and industry players that were at the forefront of this drive (CHM 2019). Their interest was not to enable e-government service delivery but to advance research and for the industry player to make a profit. Nevertheless, their effort led to the evolution of the computer in such a way that it enabled more G2C and G2B services. Furthermore, their effort led to the emergence of 3rd generation computers.

When 3rd generation computers emerged, these computers were far smaller than the 2nd generation computers and worked with integrated circuits (Steitz 2006). Today, third generation computers have evolved to becoming PCs and mobile computers. The difference between early third generation computers and 2nd generation computers was being equipped with magnetic storage and later, databases. Magnetic storage enabled the possibility of processing and storage of data (CHM 2019). Databases on the other hand allowed for easy access and manipulation of data (Foote 2017). Over time, with the advent of the personal computer in the 1970s until today, computer applications utilized to create, process, analyse and transmit data have evolved. As a result, the evolution of 3rd generation computers has opened up more opportunities for the creation, storage and processing of citizen data and business data needed to assess and provide improvement to government service delivery.

Following these timelines from the 1960s to the 1970s onwards, it is evident that government agencies in, for example European countries, the US and Japan among other developed countries, were adopting computers for G2G and G2E service delivery processes (Price and Mulvihill 1965) (Kokai 1974). In the same manner, there was a growing influence of institutions on the adoption processes at the service delivery level. Hitherto, societal institutions governed the process. But between the 1960s through the 70s these societal institutions, though established, were not enough to modify the service delivery processes due to regulative mandates inhibiting those modifications. Hence, in Europe, laws had to be changed to legitimize the use of computers not just for data processing, but for the support in legislative processes (Kokai 1974). This is because the volume of information processed provided insights that could support legislation and information management. This was information gathered from businesses, citizens, government agencies etc.

These institutions became necessary as a result of the advance in technology that could actually facilitate e-government service delivery. For example, aside from the capabilities of 3rd generation computers, inspired by the telex, the internet (then known as ARPANET) and peer-to-peer messaging (email) protocols were developed in the 1960s (CHM 2019). The ARPANET was used by the military, but email was utilized by government agencies for messages. Furthermore, by the 1970s, technical capabilities that would result in future web-based e-government services were invented; and peer-to-peer computer networks using Local Area Networks were developed. As a result, computers could "communicate" with one another and the operators could easily transfer files and messages. Furthermore, by the late 1960s and early 1970s, databases and application software respectively were being developed. For the application software, Microsoft and Apple led the way. These capabilities, coupled with the decreasing price (Kraemer and Dedrick 1997) and increasing ownership of computers by individuals and government agencies enabled the digitization of government processes for G2G and G2E service delivery. These developments further enabled the institutional vision towards strengthening G2G and G2E government service delivery. These technical inventions coupled with the advancement in network technology led to the evolution of e-government services in the 1980s.

As the institutions were evolving as a result of the technology, so too were international institutions emerging. In this period from the 1960s onward, most countries in the west had problems on how to successfully integrate computers in the facilitation of G2G and G2E services delivery. In order to solve the problem, it was necessary to understand the problem by sharing experiences and solving the identified problems via cross-learning of best practices on how to handle the issues. This effort resulted in the formation of the International Computation Centre (ICC), an informal forum under the auspices of UNESCO between 1962 and 1968 (ICA-it 2019). Government representatives from 13 countries were part of the first conference. Today, the organization hosts about 20 member countries from different continents. Within this context, cognitive and normative institutions via mimetic and normative isomorphism are formed. These institutions emerge via knowledge sharing of best practices at the ICA-iT conferences. The knowledge gathered in this process is transferred to the government agencies represented by the delegates to become institutionalized as the best way of handing the problems discussed. Today, this body still exists and provides policy support to policy makers on how to facilitate and implement IT policies to promote efficiency and effectiveness of governments (ibid). This forum is one among many.

Therefore in the 1960s and 70s, there was a continuous mutual interaction between institutions, government services and the technology. As the technologies changed, so did institutions and government services. Furthermore, as technologies evolved, societal and agency institutions seemed to be insufficient, hence there was the need for international institutions.

4.2.4. Age of the Personal Computers (PC)

In the previous periods the interaction between the institution, government service and ICT was developing. Hence, the interaction between the three were not always mutual as discussed earlier. However, from the 1980s onward, there was a change. The change was triggered not only by network technologies; the new 3rd generation computer capabilities as mentioned earlier; but also by the evolution of the 3rd generation computers to PCs. PCs were not only smaller, had greater capacity and functionality, but citizens could acquire them and governments could deploy them to facilitate digital G2E and G2B services. These possibilities triggered the emergence of national and international institutions that have greatly influenced the use of technology to facilitate government service delivery.

At the national level, based on the usefulness to service delivery presented by the computer, countries such as Cyprus, Singapore and Norway launched early normative institutional policies aimed at facilitating e-government services in the 1980s (Christodoulou 2007) (OECD 2005) (Birger, Lee and Goh 2008) . These policies were directed at specific services to which the technology (computer) would play a role in the service delivery process. Some countries did go ahead to implement some of these initiatives using existing computer and telecom network technology. For example in Europe, Minitel, Teletex and videotext, CompuServe provided the possibility of developing terminals to some G2B and G2C services (Campbell-Kelly 2018). The same was the case in South America. By the 1990s until the 2000s, the adoption of computers and network technologies for G2B and G2G service delivery in the West and in South America was growing (Porrua 2013). Hence, the remote delivery of government services to customers and businesses using computers was emerging. Technology readiness and the remodeling of the national institutional frameworks drove this emergence.

Still, at the national level, as the usefulness of PCs coupled with the commercialization of the internet increased, so did more national normative ICT policies emerge. These policies, just as previous policies identified the computer and network technologies as the best tools towards facilitating digital government services. Therefore, to achieve this aim, it was necessary to revamp the mode of service delivery to citizens, employees, businesses and governments. These policies had a two-staged prescription for this digital service delivery remodeling process. The first stage of such policies was to ensure the digitization of the service delivery process (horizontal service). The second stage was to ensure that the different computer systems facilitating different services are interoperable (vertical service) (Pardo, Nam and Brian 2013). The result of these initiatives would be that a country would provide a digital one-stop shop for the citizen, business, government agency and government employees. By the 1990s, countries in Europe had implemented the first stage. The second stage by the turn of the 21st century by more countries with Japan and South Korea as forerunners. In some countries, both stages were planned and designed as national-centric portals, while in other countries the citizen-centric design approaches were adopted for the e-government portal. Nevertheless, in recent times, there is a great deal of interest in the citizen centric approach as mentioned earlier. Hence, how government services were delivered evolved for the first time in centuries. The services were becoming more technology reliant. Furthermore, the personal face-to-face and telephone interaction between government agents and either citizens, businesses and their colleagues was replaced with non-personal interactions. This proceeds until today.

At the international level, in the 1990s a new form of e-government service delivery was envisioned by the European Union (Williams, Falch and Tadayoni 2018). This new form of service delivery was the cross-border e-government service. Here, foreign citizens and businesses are able to access government services in another country. Examples include immigration services, filing of US related IRS taxes, business registration etc. The regional institutions created by the European Union drove this envisioned form of e-government service delivery, which is being realized now see (CEF 2018). In the same vain, government agencies are also able to collaborate under bilateral institutional frameworks in order to solve crime, facilitate economic development and even conduct bilateral government meetings at the comfort of their offices without having to travel. In the EU, national institutions are being harmonized with the regional institutions to enable this new approach to government service delivery. This is necessary; or else it will be illegitimate to enforce regional institutional initiatives, unless they are EU regulative institutions. If not, member states have to harmonize their laws. Although these are EU institutions, the member states create them or else proposed technologies and services would be illegitimate. Hence, there is also an interaction between institutions, government services and technology in this process.

Aside from EU and bilateral initiatives at the international level, the technological possibility posed by PCs and network technologies has resulted in more coordinated regional initiatives. These initiatives are UN driven initiatives. One of the UN initiatives is in Africa. A UN agency, the Economic Commission for Africa (ECA) has facilitated normative institutional frameworks via the AISI. They have further embarked on change management initiatives that have resulted in African countries developing normative institutional policies in the 1990s and 2000s (Hafkin 2009). These policies are similar and possessed a two-pronged approach. The first was to enable businesses, citizens have access to ICT, and the second was to equip government with the institutions and technology to deliver e-government services. These policies are the basis for the development of e-government initiatives in Africa. The World Bank and other international development agencies have had to support these initiatives either financially or with technical resources. The challenge however, is that the regulative institutions governing government agencies providing the government services are at odds with the e-government policies in Africa. Hence, it is a bit challenging to implement some of the new ideas in the different e-government related policies.

Other UN organization promoting e-government institutions globally include, the United Nations Economic and Social Council (ECOSOC) and the Division of a Public Administration and Development Management

(DPAPM) of the United Nations Department of Economic and Social Affairs (UN-DESA). UN-DESA publishes a bi-annual e-government survey which began in 2016 that has not only defined e-government but provided criteria on what should be in place and a yardstick for measuring e-government performance of each country (for example (UNPAN 2016)). Although these measures are not regulative yardsticks, they have over time evolved into normative institutions by which policy makers and researchers alike use to access the e-government performance of countries. Furthermore, some policy makers have used these measures to mimic their e-government delivery approaches.

Based on these examples, it is evident that the possibilities presented by the personal computer and network technologies has triggered institutional frameworks to frame new ways and approaches towards the delivery of government services. Hence, in this case the mutual interaction between the three elements is evident.

5. THE THREE ELEMENTS AND FUTURE E-GOVERNMENT SERVICES

So what does the future hold? In the previous section, an effort provided examples from history and from contemporary times on the mutual influence between technology, government services and institutions. These institutions were either societal, international, national or agency institutions. This finding does have a practical implication to the adoption of e-government services in the future. These implications can be deduced from the trend of examples provided in the previous section. The obvious implication is that future e-government services will be cross-border services; driven by future technologies; and governed by the harmonization of national and international institutions. The international institutions need not be regulative. That is not to imply that it is not possible. Nevertheless, in this chapter the power of cognitive institutions has been revealed, so cognitive institutions could as well form the basis of an international e-government order. In such an order, different countries control their systems, but mimic each other as a means of facilitating international technical and operational interoperability. In some way that is happening now and is bound to continue.

Future e-government services will be necessitated by growth in cross-border trade, the growth in migration, the growth in government-to-government cross-border cooperation, and the growth in e-commerce. These are necessities laden with potential cross-border G2G, G2B, and G2G services. The necessities are currently driving emerging global economy and globalization as well. Hence, countries around the globe rely more and more on each other than ever before. They rely on each other for all kinds of resources, which supports their economic growth. Therefore different countries and regions around the globe are either likely to copy the footsteps of the EU or adopt similar initiatives that will enable cross-border e-government service delivery. So far, there is a move in this direction. For example, currently Estonia has digital citizens. These are neither residents nor citizens of Estonia, but due to the advancement in technology, Estonia has opened its government services to these digital citizens. A regulative institution of rules provided by the Estonian government backs this approach. Therefore, even though the digital citizen is not resident in Estonia, he or she is governed by the rules of the program. Hence, as discussed in this chapter, there is still that interaction between the institution, government services and technology. This therefore implies that the success of these future e-government services, necessitated by the forces of globalization will hinge on the positive mutual influence between the three elements.

Although cross-border e-government service delivery is seen as the future, the organizational entities that will drive this international process are in place. These organizational entities are already active. These entities include The African Union (AU), Association of Southeast Asian Nations (ASEAN), Union of South American nations (USAN), Council of Europe (COE), European Union (EU), League of Arab States (LAS), Organization of American States (OAS), Pacific Islands Forum (PIF) and South Asian Association for Regional Cooperation (SAARC). These organizations were established to facilitate regional cooperation and trade. Therefore, it will be in their interest to encourage cross-border e-government services among their member states as a way of achieving their vision. As a fact, some of these organizations, such as the EU and AU, have established legislative and judicial bodies who are and can respectively facilitate cross-border e-government services. Other organizations may follow suit or adopt different approaches towards achieving the same goal. Although these differences in institutional approach might occur, they will also have to agree on regional technical standards for their systems and the government services that will help them achieve their regional objectives.

Aside from the initiatives or regional organizational entities, agencies of the United Nations will also play a significant role. As mentioned earlier, the United Nations Economic and Social Council (ECOSOC) are playing an important role in the process. The do this via their resolutions on e-government (UN Library 1995) and their agencies. These resolutions are not chapter 7 resolutions and hence non-binding on member states. However, they are not wasted because regional UN Economic Commissions such as the Economic Commission for Africa (UNECA) and the Economic Commission for Asia and the Pacific (UNESCAP) implement ECOSOC resolutions. They also galvanize government leaders in their respective region to create resolutions, legislative mandates and resolutions. Then national agencies in partnership with the Economic Commissions will then institutionalize these mandates in their respective countries and adopt them (see (UNESCAP 2013) (ECA 1996) (UNECA 2017)). The institutions created by ECOSOC are normative, while the economic commission in partnership with member states can create regulative institutions. Nevertheless, these relationships are bound to continue in future. The outcome, if successful, will be the establishment of a cognitive institution governing global cross-border e-government service delivery. But as it is, it is likely that that might be farfetched for the foreseeable future. The main reason is because the institutions they rely on and try to promote are often not compatible with the existing government services. But they are more successful in helping different member states implement the necessary technology. Therefore, since the interplay between their institutions, the present government services and technology is problematic, hence they are not very successful as compared to regional organizations such as the EU. However, this does not imply that they will not get this right in the future as well as play a more significant role in cross-border e-government delivery.

Just as international organizations are in place to facilitate future cross-border e-government services, so are national governments in Europe, Asia and the Middle East. These governments have begun the creation of normative institutions that will adopt future technologies such as artificial intelligence to facilitate e-government services. These countries include - Canada, Japan, Singapore, China, the UAE, and Finland - who adopted their policies in 2017 and Denmark, France, the UK, South Korea, and India who adopted theirs in 2018 (Dutton 2018). The EU, although not a country, adopted theirs in 2018 (ibid). The e-government section of these policies are referred to as AI in government. These normative institutions are nascent and are aimed at enhancing the delivery of government services using data driven algorithms. This idea is necessitated by the fact that currently in some EU countries such as Denmark, Sweden, citizens and businesses can perform e-government transactions without the intervention of government agents. Government agents working at the back end of the system only process the transactions. Hence, based on these possibilities, AI is to be adopted to take the government service delivery process further. AI will enable end-to-end machine transaction process. This implies that the processing of the transactions will be automated. However, on careful observation, it is evident that the national agencies facilitating these institutions are utilizing AI (technology) to create AI compatible government services – hence that interplay between government services, technology and institutions.

These initiatives are currently proposed for national e-government services. However, as explained earlier, globalization will 'force' government agencies to look for ways of facilitating cross-border e-government services using this technology. Either such initiatives, depending on the institutions governing the process might be solo individual efforts such as the current Estonian e-residency initiative or the facilitation of the mutual interoperability of national infrastructures as promoted in the EU. Whichever way it ends up being, there will be cross-border e-government services. Furthermore, such services will be enabled by the interplay between institutions, the technology and the government services in question.

DISCUSSION AND CONCLUSION

The chapter has identified examples of how the interaction between government services, technology and institutions shaped e-government service delivery over the years and for the near future. There have also been examples, which indicate that e-government service delivery is hampered when this interplay does not exist. Hence, it is safe to say that the suspicions that led to the study reported here were confirmed. Obviously, that is the reason this chapter was reported, or else there would be no need to report this finding, as it would have no practical significance.

Nevertheless, as it is, there is a practical significance to this finding. The revelation of the role of the three elements on the delivery of government services arms government agencies with a framework towards assessing if they have all they need to facilitate a particular e-government service. Furthermore, it also helps government agencies understand areas they need to consider if they have to diagnose why the facilitation of a particular e-government service is failing.

Another practical significance was from a surprise finding. What was surprising in the course of drafting this chapter was how cognitive societal institutions influenced the adoption and delivery of specific e-government services. This surprise resulted in the first publication (Williams, Falch and Tadayoni 2018). But as the investigation was made into historical examples, it was glaring that initial cognitive institutions played a greater role in influencing government services and the technology to be adopted much more than regulative and normative institutions. In most cases, it was the precursor to regulative and normative institutions. This actually implies that policy makers implementing specific e-government services should not overlook the cognitive institutions governing the adoption of the technology in society. If government agents working in a government agency have already adopted a shared understanding of the usefulness of a technology to their task that will influence the decision to adopt or oppose the technology.

Another issue of practical significance, which was not a surprise finding, is the need for government agencies to determine if existing institutions are sufficiently facilitating a particular e-government service. In some cases, societal institutions are sufficient, for example in the use of AI etc. But in most cases, it is necessary to find out the proposed service needs of a regulative institution in order to enable its adoption by government agencies. This is especially important if there are regulative rules on how the service should be delivered. In other cases, deregulation may be required but a normative institution might be relevant. For example, it might not be expedient to make the adoption of certain technologies for the delivery of an e-government service mandatory. This is because technologies evolve and if a new technology emerges, this regulation will become a bottleneck. Hence, granting government institutions the rights to adopt technologies that enhances the service might be a better approach. Hence, the norm would be that all government services should be digital. Nevertheless, how this norm will be implemented could be left for agencies.

The final practical issue is based on the observation that jurisdictions, where particular e-government service deliveries were successful, were those with living institutions. Living institutions here imply institutions that were not static, but evolving alongside technology. Hence, national governments need organizational frameworks that will enable institutional evolution. The framework could be the adoption of a bottom-up approach in the proposal of institutions by government agencies. Such an approach could be supplemented with occasional surveys to government agencies, finding out if there is the need for institutional change to support the e-delivery of their services.

In conclusion, this chapter was inspired by practice, even though there has been an attempt to present it in an academic perspective. However, that does not imply that the chapter does not have implications for research as well. From an academic perspective, what would be of interest could be the empirical testing of the weight of each element in the relationship and to further find out if such an outcome is generalizable. That was not possible from the approach adopted in this book. But it is very likely that each element does not carry equal weight. But there is the possibility that predictions on the possibility of government service being digitized if each of the element possesses certain weight.

REFERENCES

Agar, J. 2003. *The Government Machine: A Revolutionary History of the Computer*. Cambridge, MA: MIT Press,.

Bauby, P, MM Simile, and P Raimbault. 2010. *Mapping of the Public Service - Public Services in the European Union and in the 27 Member States - Statistics, Organization and Regulations*. May. https://www.ceep.eu/images/stories/pdf/Mapping/CEEP_mapping%20experts%20report.pdf.

Berthold, VM. 1922. *History of the Telephone and Telegraph in Brazil 1851 - 1921*. Michigan: the University of Michigan.

Birger, F, SK Lee, and CB Goh. 2008. *Towards a Better Future: Education and Training for Economic Development in Singapore since 1965*. Washington: World Bank Publications,.

Blondheim, M. 1994. *News Over the Wires: The Telegraph and the Flow of Public Information in America, 1844-1897*. Harvard University Press.

Boyce, RW. 2000. "Imperial Dreams and National Realities: Britain, Canada and the Struggle for a Pacific Telegraph Cable, 1879-1902." *The English Historical Review* 115 (460): 39-70.

Calhoun, ES. 1956. "New computer developments around the world." *Proceedings in AIEE-IRE '56 (Eastern) Papers and discussions presented at the December 10-12, 1956, eastern joint computer conference: New developments in computers.* New York: ACM. 5 - 9.

Campbell-Kelly, M. 2018. *Computer, Student Economy Edition: A History of the Information Machine.* Routledge.

Carré, PA. 1993. "From the telegraph to the telex: a history of technology, early networks and issues in France in the 19th and 20th centuries." *FLUX Cahiers scientifiques internationaux Réseaux et Territoires* 11: 17- 31.

CEF. 2018. *Connecting Europe Facility.* https://ec.europa.eu/cefdigital/wiki/display/CEFDIGITAL/About+CEF+building+blocks.

Census.gov (a). 2018. *UNIVAC 1.* https://www.census.gov/history/www/innovations/technology/univac_i.html.

Census.gov. 2018. *United States Census Bureau.* August 1. https://www.census.gov/history/www/innovations/technology/tabulation_and_processing.html.

CHM. 2019. *Computer History Museum.* https://www.computerhistory.org/timeline/1951/.

Choudhury, DK. 2010. "Of Codes and Coda: Meaning in Telegraph Messages, circa 1850-1920." *Historical Social Research / Historische Sozialforschung* 35 (1 (131)): 127-139.

Christodoulou, E. 2007. "Cyprus." In *EU Enlargement: Economic Development and the Information Society*, by G Ţurlea, 47 - 74. Asp / Vubpress / Upa.

CIA.gov. 1968. *US Government Correspondence manual.* https://www.cia.gov/library/readingroom/docs/CIA-RDP74-00005R000200060043-0.pdf.

Clark, W. 1896. "Constitutional changes which are foreshadowed." *American Law Review* 30 (5): 702 - 709.

Clark, W. 1895. "The legal aspect of the Telegraph and the telephone: Essential parts of an efficient postal service." *American Law Review* 29: 675-680.

Clayton, J. 1997. "The Voice in the Machine." In *Language Machines: Technologies of Literary and Cultural Production*, by J Masten, P Stallybrass and N Vicker. Psychology Press.

Cortada, JW. 2007. *The Digital Hand, Vol 3: How Computers Changed the Work of American Public Sector Industries, Volume 3.* Oxford University Press.

Derdak, T, and A Hast. 1992. *International Directory of Compnay Histories.* Michigan: St James Press.

DIGST. 2019. *Agency for Digitization.* https://en.digst.dk/policy-and-strategy/mandatory-digitisation/digital-post/.

Dimaggio, PJ, and WW Powell. 1983. "The Iron Cage revisited: Institutional isomorphism and the collective rationality in Organizational Fields." *American Sociological Review* 48 (2): 147-160.

Dutton, A. 2018. "AI Policy 101: An Introduction to the 10 Key Aspects of AI Policy." *Medium.* July 5. https://medium.com/politics-ai/ai-policy-101-what-you-need-to-know-about-ai-policy-163a2bd68d65.

ECA. 1996. *The African Information Society Initiative (AISI) - A decade's perspective.* United Nations Economic Commission for Africa.

Elon University. 2019. "1870s to 1940s Telephone." *Imagining the Internet - A History and Forecast.* https://www.elon.edu/e-web/predictions/150/1870.xhtml.

Engel, JA. 2007. "A shrinking world." In *A Companion to International History 1900 - 2001*, by G Martel, 52-64. Malden: Blackwell Publishing.

Eom, S. 2012. "Institutional Dimensions of e-Government Development: Implementing the Business Reference Model in the United States and Korea." *Administration and Society* 45 (7): 875 - 907.

Fang, Z. 2002. "E-government in Digital Era: concapts practice and development." *International Journal of the Computer* 10 (2): 1-22.

Fontain, J. 2001. *Building the Virtual State: Information Technology and Institutional Change.* Washington, D.C.: Brookings Institution Press.

Foote, KD. 2017. "Dataversity." *A Brief History of Database Management.* March 23. https://www.dataversity.net/brief-history-database-management/#.

Green, N. 1883. "The Government and the Telegraph." *The North American Review* 137 (324): 422-434.

Grönlund, A, and TA Horan. 2005. "Introducing e-Gov: History, Definitions, and Issues." *Communications of the Association for Information Systems* 15 (39): 713 - 729.

Hafkin, NJ. 2009. "E-government in Africa: Progress made and challenges ahead." *Conference on Electronic/Mobile Government in Africa: Building Capacity in Knowledge Management through Partnership, Addis Ababa, Ethiopia, 17-19 February, 2009.* Addis Ababa. http://unpan1.un.org/intradoc/groups/public/documents/un/unpan0335 26.pdf.

Hall, BH, and B Khan. 2002. "Adoption of new technology." In *New Economy Handbook*, by D C Jones. Academic Press, San Diego,.

Hanna, NK. 2010. "Government Transformation: Vision and Journey." In *e-Transformation: Enabling New Development Strategies. Innovation, Technology, and Knowledge Management*, by N K Hanna, 251-280. IGI global.

Heinze, N, and Q Hu. 2005. "E-Government Research: A Review via the Lens of Structuration Theory." *Conference: Pacific Asia Conference on Information Systems, PACIS 2005, Bangkok, Thailand, July 7-10, 2005.* Bangkok,: DBLP.

Higgs, R. 2008. "Government Growth." In *Concise Economics (2nd Ed)*, by D R Henderson. Indianapolis: Library of Economics and Liberty.

Highton, E. 1852. *The Electric Telegraph; Its History and Progress by Edward Highton.* J. Weale,.

Holcombe, AN. 1906. "The Telephone in Great Britain." *The Quarterly Journal of Economics* (The Quarterly Journal of Economics) 21 (1): 96-135.

Hollerith, H. 1894. "The Electrical Tabulating Machine." *Journal of the Royal Statistical Society* 57 (4): 678 - 689.

House.gov. 2019. *'What hath God Wrought' The House and the Telegraph.* https://history.house.gov/Exhibitions-and-Publications/Electronic-Technology/Telegraph/.

Hubbard, GG. 1883. "Government Control of the Telegraph." *The North American Review* (University of Northern Iowa) 137 (325): 521 -535.

ICA-it. 2019. "ICA Connecting CIOs, Enriching Governments." *ICA-iT.* https://www.ica-it.org/index.php/about-us/history-of-the-ica.

ITU. 2019. "ITU Statistics." *International Telecommunications Union.* https://www.itu.int/en/ITU-D/Statistics/Pages/stat/default.aspx.

Kim, S, HJ Kim, and H Lee. 2009. "An institutional analysis of an e-government system for anti-corruption: The case of OPEN." *Government Information Quaterly* 26 (1): 42-50.

Knuesel, A. 2017. "British Diplomacy and the Telegraph in Nineteenth-Century China." *Diplomacy and Statecraft* 18 (2007): 517-537.

Koenig, D. 1944. "Telegraphs and Telegrams in Revolutionary France." *The Scientific Monthly* 59 (6): 431-437.

Kokai, TR. 1974. "Measures towards EDP- Appropriate legislation." *Jurimetrics Journal* 15 (37): 37 - 42.

Kraemer, KL, and J Dedrick. 1997. "Computing and Public Organizations." *Journal of Public Administration Research and Theory: J-PART* 7 (1): 89-112.

Laning, CB. 1965. "Forces and trends in State and Local Government EDP." *Public Administration Review* 25 (2): 151- 155.

Lemon, WF, SH Holden, and JJ Preece. 2003. "A descriptive Framework for Federal Electronic Government: A Necessary step prior to field." In *Information Technology and Organizations: Trends, Issues, Challenges and Solutions, Volume 1,* by M Khosrowpour, 359 - 362. IGI Global.

Lindley, L. 1971. *The Constitution Faces Technology: The Relationship of the National Government to the Telegraph, 1866 - 1884.* Houston: Rice University.

Lubar, S. 1991. ""Do not fold, spindle or mutilate": A cultural history of the punch card." *Landley.net.* May. https://www.landley.net/history/mirror/pre/fsm.html.

Manoharan, AP, and A Ingrams. 2018. "Conceptualizing E-Government from Local Government Perspectives." *State and Local Government Review* 50 (1): 56-66.

Martin, C. 2017. *Alexander Graham Bell and the 1900 Census.* 3. https://www.census.gov/history/pdf/agbellarticle-32017.pdf.

Martland, SJ. 2014. "Standardizing the state while integrating the frontier: the Chilean telegraph system in the Araucanía, 1870-1900." *History and Technology* 30 (4): 283 - 308.

Merrill, J. 2019. *May 10-President Hayes has first telephone installed in the White house.* http://www.touringohio.com/history/event/may-10-president-hayes-has-first-telephone-installed-in-the-white-house/.

Morse, SF. 1914. *American Jupiter: Letters and Journals of Samuel F.B. Morse (Vol. I & II).* Big Byte Books.

Nonberg, AL. 1990. "High-Technology Calculation in the Early 20th Century: Punched Card Machinery in Business and Government." *Technology and Culture* 31 (4): 753 - 779.

Nonnenmacher, T. 2019. "History of the U.S. Telegraph Industry." *Economic History Services.* https://eh.net/encyclopedia/history-of-the-u-s-telegraph-industry/.

North, Douglass C. 1990. *Institutions, Institutional Change and Economic Performance.* Cambridge: Cambridge university press.

OECD. 2005. *Volume 2005 of OECD e-Government Studies.* OECD.

Oliver, RL. 1980. "A Cognitive Model of the Antecedents and Consequences of Satisfaction Decisions." *Journal of Marketing Research* 17 (4): 460.

Pardo, TA, T Nam, and BC Brian. 2013. "E-Government Interoperability." *Social Science Computer Review* 30 (1): 7-23.

Patil, CS, RR Karhe, and MA Aher. 2012. "Review on Generations in Mobile Cellular Technology." *International Journal of Emerging Technology and Advanced Engineering* 2 (10): 614-619.

Porrua, MA. 2013. "E-government in Latin America: A Review of the Success in Colombia, Uruguay and Panama." In *The Global Information Technology Report 2013 - Growth and Jobs in a Hyperconnected World*, by B Bilbao-Osorio, S Dutta and B Lanvin, 127 -136. World Economic Forum.

Price, DG, and DE Mulvihill. 1965. "The Present and Future Use of Computers in State Government." *Public Administration Review* 25 (2): 142-150.

Quevedo, JM. 2010. "Telecommunications and Colonial Rivalry: European Telegraph Cables to the Canary Islands and Northwest Africa,." *Historical Social Research/Historische Sozialforschung* 35 (1 (131)): 108-124.

Regeringskansliet. 2011. *ICT for Everyone - A digital Agenda for Sweden.* Stockholm: Ministry of Enterprise, Energy and Communications.

Richie, RW, and WE Alli. 1960. "Office Automation in the Federal Government." *Monthly Labor review* 83 (9): 933-938.

Rogers, R, and J Reardon. 1999. *Recommendations for International Action: Barriers to a Global Information Society for Health.* IOS Press.

Salifu-Siddi, F, and I Williams. 2016. "The challenges of replicating Western E-government Structures in Ghana." *The 1st Africa Regional ITS Conference in Accra, Ghana, March 10-11. 2016.* Accra: ITS.

Savas, ES. 1978. "The Institutional Structure of Local Government Services: A Conceptual Model." *Public Administration Review* 38 (5): 412-419.

Scott, WR. 1995. *Institutions and Organizations.* Thousand Oaks: Sage.

Silock, R. 2001. "What is e-government." *Parliamentary Affairs* 54 (1): 88-101.

SMG. 2019. *National Telephone Company directory, 1898-1899.* National Telephone Company directory, 1898-1899.

Smith, JQ. 1877. "Instructions relating to Official Correspondence by mail and telegraph." *Yakima Memory.* August 21. https://archives.yvl.org/handle/20.500.11867/3759.

Smith, RM. 1889. "Sketch of the history of telegraphic communication between the United Kingdom and India." *Scottish Geographical Magazine* 5 (1): 1-11.

Sott, WR. 2001. *Institutions and organizations.* Thousand Oaks: Sage publications.

Steitz, B. 2006. *Boston University.* http://people.bu.edu/baws/brief%20computer%20history.html.

The Sydney Morning herald. 1878. *Private Telegraphs.* April 19.

UN Library. 1995. "Index to proceedings of the Economic and Social Council - organizational session 1992." *UN library.* https://library.un.org/sites/library.un.org/files/itp/1430-201404101437575267777_0.pdf.

UNECA. 2017. *UNECA Mandates.* https://www.uneca.org/pages/mandates.

UNESCAP. 2013. "Resolution 69/10 Promoting regional information and communications technology connectivity and building knowledge-networked societies in Asia and the Pacific." *United Nations Economic and Social Commission for Asia.* May 1. https://www.unescap.org/sites/default/files/69-10_0.pdf.

UNPAN . 2016. *United Nations E-government Survey 2016.* New York: UN.

US Congress. 1960. *Report on the use of electronic data-processing equipment in the federal government.* Washington. https://www.actiac.org/system/files/Congressional%20hearing%20from%201960%20listing%20all%20524%20government%20computers.pdf.

US Congress. 1989. *SSA's Toll-free Telephone System: Service Or Disservice? : Hearing Before the Special Committee on Aging, United States Senate, One Hundred First Congress, First Session, Washington, DC, April 10, 1989, Volume 4.* Washington: U.S. Government Printing Office.

Weerakkodya, V, R El-Haddadeh, U Sivarajah, A Omar, and A Molnar. 2019. "A case analysis of E-government service delivery through a service chain dimension." *International Journal of Information Management* 47 (2019): 233-238.

Wells, DA. 1873. *The Relation of the Government to the Telegraph.* University of Michigan.

West, DM. 2004. "E-Government and the Transformation of ServiceDelivery and Citizen Attitudes." *Public administration Review* 64 (1): 15-27.

Williams, I. 2015. *Analysis of Public Private Interplay Frameworks in the Development of Rural Telecommunications Infrastructure: A Multiple-Case Study.* Aalborg: Aalborg University Press.

Williams, I, M Falch, and R Tadayoni. 2018. "Institutional Legitimacy and Digital Public Cross-Border Service Delivery between Denmark/Sweden and Denmark/Germany." *Journal of NBICT* 1 (2018): 1-30.

Williams, I, M Falch, and R Tadayoni. 2018. "Internationalization of e-Government Services." *11th CMI International Conference: Prospects and Challenges Towards Developing a Digital Economy within the EU, 29–30 NOVEMBER 2018.* Copenhagen Denmark: IEEE. 19-31.

Williamsom, O. 2000. "The 'New Institutional Economics: Taking Stock, Looking Ahead." *Journal of Economic Literature* XXXVIII: 595–613.

World Bank. 2016. *World Development Report 2016 - Digital dividends.* Washington: World Bank Group.

Worldbank. 2011. "E-government." *World bank Web Archive.* https://www.worldbank.org/en/webarchives/archive?url=httpzzxxweb.worldbank.org/archive/website01358/WEB/0__MENUP.HTM&mdk=23350751.

Wright, C. 1900. *Census.gov.* https://www.census.gov/history/pdf/wright-hunt.pdf.

Yang, D. 1996. *The Technology of Japanese Imperialism: Telecommunications and Empire-Building, 1895-1945.* Havard University.

Young, JR. 1890. "American Influence in China." *The North American Review* 151 (405): 192-200.

In: E-Government
Editor: Anil Sieben

ISBN: 978-1-53617-563-9
© 2020 Nova Science Publishers, Inc.

Chapter 2

ENTERPRISE ARCHITECTURES IN THE LOCAL E-GOVERNMENT CONTEXT: A SYSTEMATIC LITERATURE MAPPING

Daniela Gallegos-Baeza, Ignacio Velásquez, Angélica Caro* *and Alfonso Rodríguez*
Computer Science and Information Technologies Department,
University of Bío-Bío, Chillán, Chile

ABSTRACT

Nowadays, governments increasingly use Information and Communication Technologies, both for supporting their internal processes and for providing products and services to citizens and the industry. This style of government is known as e-government. An important advantage of e-government is that it provides the potential to improve the efficiency of processes and the scope of governmental services. This is especially fundamental in the context of local governments, or municipalities, as they are relevant participants in the well-being of citizens and in the development of their corresponding

---

* Corresponding Author's E-mail: mcaro@ubiobio.cl.

communities. This is because municipalities are the governmental entity that is closest to the community and that generates the greatest impact on it. Thus, the incorporation of technology must be consistent with the objectives of municipalities and its efficacy must be constantly assessed by the citizens. To achieve this, being able to visualize the existing alignment between the objectives, services, processes and supporting technology becomes essential. This would allow to more adequately approach, through the support of information technologies, the constant evolution that is confronted in municipal management.

A strategy to accomplish the above is the creation of the municipality's Enterprise Architecture. An Enterprise Architecture provides a holistic view of an organization. This allows identifying its motivational components, as well as the processes, services and supporting technology, the relationships of these components and the principles of the organization's design and evolution. In the last years, they have recurrently been proposed as a framework for e-government initiatives and as a means for obtaining standardization, convergence and interoperability. Due to this, the interest to learn what is the adoption level of Enterprise Architectures in municipalities across the world arises.

Thus, this chapter focuses on presenting the results of a systematic literature mapping that reviews the adoption level of enterprise architectures in local e-governments. These results will allow to learn where and how have Enterprise Architectures been used, to see what frameworks are used for their definition, and to identify possible challenges and opportunities for their utilization in the local e-government context.

Keywords: enterprise architecture, municipal e-government, systematic literature mapping

INTRODUCTION

A municipality (or local government) is a fundamental organization for the realization of the community. Its goal is to provide services that guarantee the participation of citizens in the economic, social and cultural progress (Grossi and Reichard 2016; Vakkala and Leinonen 2020). In the context of Electronic Government (e-government), municipalities acquire relevance as they are the closest public organizations to the citizens while also being the one that provides the most services directly to them

(Sandoval Almazan and Mendoza Colin 2011). Due to this closeness to the citizens, the trend is for them to readily stay in contact, for example, through the information and services that they provide, while being supported by technological platforms.

Nowadays, local governments have become the providers of a variety of services. Here, the use of online systems and Information and Communication Technologies (ICT) has allowed the continuous provision of these services throughout the day (Navarro, Cañavate, and Bleda 2008).

Likewise, the use of ICT in e-government must be constantly assessed and measured to determine the real benefits that are being provided to the citizenship (Batlle Montserrat, Abadal, and Blat 2011). For this, having an explicitly evidenced global view of how the motivational aspects of a municipality relate with its processes, services and supporting technology becomes fundamental.

On the other hand, Enterprise Architectures (EA), which are defined as an instrument for directing and integrating ICT for the whole enterprise (Lankhorst, Proper, and Jonkers 2010), have been suggested as a framework for electronic management initiatives and as a roadmap to follow for achieving standardization, convergence and interoperability in local governments. This is because EA allow the possibility of obtaining a holistic view of the local government, including the information, the people and the technology (Ask and Hedström 2011; Hornnes, Jansen, and Langeland 2010).

Thus, the research interest of this study is to learn the use of EA in the context of local e-government throughout the world, their level of adoption and the frameworks and notations that are utilized to model these architectures. Consequently, this study focuses on identifying and cataloguing the bibliographic material that address this topic through the realization of a Systematic Literature Mapping (SLM) (Kitchenham et al. 2009) as the research methodology.

The remainder of this chapter is organized as follows. The main concepts related to this study are presented in Section 2. The planning and realization of the SLM are presented in Section 3, whereas its results shown in Section 4. Section 5 provides a discussion of the results of the SLM. Finally, the conclusion and future work are presented in Section 5.

BACKGROUND

The main concepts that are addressed in this research are defined in this section. These concepts are e-Government and Enterprise Architectures.

E-Government

The e-government is one of the most interesting topics that have been introduced in the field of public management in the late 90s (Moon 2002). In general, it can be described as the use of ICT by the government, with the objective of providing services to citizens, enterprises and other entities through the web.

Although various definitions of e-government can be found, three relatively extensive definitions are shown next: (i) utilization of ICT in public management's tasks and processes, with the objective of changing the relation between the government and the citizens regarding the provision of public services, internal efficiency and the improvement of citizen participation (Batlle Montserrat, Abadal, and Blat 2011); (ii) e-government addresses the improvement of public services, governance and democracy through the development of approaches centered on the client, and the improvement of internal and external relations by using ICT (Paiva Dias 2011) and (iii) e-government corresponds to the use of ICT for allowing and improving the efficiency of governmental services that are offered to the citizens, employees and enterprises (Carter and Bélanger 2005).

The use of e-government allows to improve the governmental management. It propels a substantial modification of the work style, utilizing technologies not only for the automatization of the traditional management styles, but also for transforming them. Likewise, it provides direct benefits to the general public, such as the elimination of time and space barriers, an easiness in communications, transparency, equality in the access to information, availability of governmental information, reduction of costs, and the increase in the production of goods and services. All of this with the aim of a better quality of life for the citizenship (Sandoval Almazan and Mendoza Colin 2011; Zuiderhoek et al. 2006).

The closest relation between the government and the citizenship is stablished through municipalities (Sandoval Almazan and Mendoza Colin 2011). Nowadays, municipalities have become the providers of a variety of services, where the use of online systems and ICT allows a continuous service the whole day (Navarro, Cañavate, and Bleda 2008).

Finally, it is important to highlight that the provision of services through e-government cannot be conceived without considering the processes that coordinate the governmental actions that produce them, the information systems that sustain them and the technological infrastructure that ensures their viability and sustainability (Poggi 2013).

Enterprise Architecture

An Enterprise Architecture is an instrument for directing and integrating the whole enterprise, helping to guide and to optimize the ICT investments of the organization and allowing to translate commercial strategies into technological solutions that can be implemented (Lankhorst, Proper, and Jonkers 2010). EA are supported by principles, methods and models that are utilized for the design and realization of an enterprises organizational structure, its business processes, information systems and infrastructure (The Open Group 2017).

The most important applications of an EA are (i) the analysis of problems in the current state of an enterprise (known as the As Is state), (ii) determining its desired future state (known as the To Be state), and (iii) assuring that the development projects in the transformation programs are in accordance with the desired To Be states. This implies that, in an EA model, coherence and a general view are more important than specifity and detail (Lankhorst, Proper, and Jonkers 2010).

One of the first EA frameworks that have been proposed in literature is the Zachman Framework (Zachman 1996). Here, an enterprise's components were categorized based on those that allowed to answer the questions of "what it is made of", "how it works" and "where its components are". These components would also be categorized based on the different dimensions of the enterprise: the business dimension (governance, organization and processes), the information systems dimension (data and applications) and the technology dimension (software and hardware). More recent implementations of EA frameworks may include more dimensions, but these remain the core dimensions of an EA (The Open Group 2011).

RESEARCH METHODOLOGY

The Systematic Literature Mapping (SLM) methodology has been selected for the realization of this research (Petersen, Vakkalanka, and Kuzniarz 2015). A SLM provides a global view of a topic of interest, and identifies the quantity, kind of research and available results of this topic. Likewise, it allows to identify topics where empirical evidence is scarce and more studies are required (Genero Bocco, Cruz Lemus, and Piattini Velthuis 2014).

A SLM allows objectively and rigorously studying the literature and basically consists of three stages: (i) planning, (ii) realization and (iii) presentation of results (Kitchenham et al. 2009). The rigorous application of this methodology allows reducing the risk of bias in the realization of a study and ensures the completeness of the obtained results.

This SLM has been realized in two stages, as depicted in Figure 1. The first stage took place during the first quarter of 2018 and it mapped the publications until 2017. Its results have been presented at a conference (Gallegos-Baeza et al. 2019). A second stage was carried out during the last quarter of 2019 to complement the previously obtained results with those published from 2017 onwards so that the knowledge base for this chapter would be up to date. This stage considered the adjustment of the used review planning to improve the quality of the found works. Finally, using the results obtained from both stages, an in-depth analysis has been performed and its main findings are provided in this chapter.

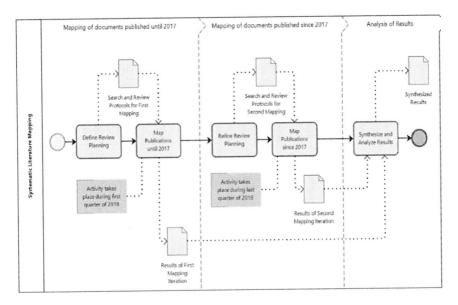

Figure 1. Process taken for the realization of the SLM.

The planning and realization stages of the SLM are described next, whereas the presentation of results is provided in the following section.

Planning of the SLM

The objective of this SLM is to study the use and adoption of enterprise architectures in local e-government. Based on this objective, the following five research Questions (Q) have been defined:

Q1: What is the level of adoption of enterprise architectures in local e-government?

Q2: What regions of the world use enterprise architectures for local e-government?

Q3: What frameworks are utilized for the creation of enterprise architectures in the context of local e-government? How has their use evolved through time?

Q4: What notations are used for modeling enterprise architectures in the context of local e-government? How has their use evolved through time?

Based on these questions, the search terms and combinations were generated for the first stage of the SLM as follows: (i) identification of the important terms from the formulated questions, (ii) inclusion of synonyms and concepts related to the identified terms, and (iii) generation of the term combinations using logical operators. For the second stage of the SLM, the utilized search terms and combinations were refined based on the experience from the searches during the first stage. Table 1 shows the defined search terms, whereas Table 2 presents the utilized search combinations for the first stage, and Table 3 presents the combinations used for the second. Regarding the refinement of the search terms and combinations, it was observed that the term "ArchiMate" restricted the search results as it involved a specific modeling language, so it was not used during the second stage. On the other hand, by analyzing the titles of the publications found in the first stage, two commonly used related terms were identified, "Framework" and "Adoption", thus, they were used during the second stage with the objective of obtaining more accurate results. Thus, the terms marked with a * in Table 1 were used only during the first stage, whereas those marked with a ** were used only during the second stage.

Four bibliographical sources were utilized for the realization of the SLM: Springer Link, Scopus, Web of Science and Google Scholar. For each bibliographical source and for each search combination, the first 200 search results were reviewed. This was done both in the Spanish and English languages. The first was utilized as it is the native language of the authors, whereas the second is the *lingua franca* for academic publications

(Duszak and Lewkowicz 2008). The same search strategy was applied for both stages of the SLM, with the exception of the range of publication years considered for the works of both stages. Concretely, works published until 2017 were reviewed in the first stage, whereas works published from 2017 were reviewed in the second stage. The year 2017 was included in both stages to avoid missing important recently published works as not all of them might have been published during the realization of the first stage. Duplicated results from both stages were properly filtered before the realization of the analysis stage.

Table 1. Search terms of the SLM

ID	Term	ID	Term	ID	Term
T1	E-Government	T2	Electronic Government	T3	Local Government
T4	Municipality	T5	City Council	T6	Enterprise Architecture
T7	ArchiMate *	T8	Framework **	T9	Adoption **

Table 2. Search combinations during the first stage of the SLM

ID	Combination
C-1	T6 AND (T3 OR T4 OR T5) AND (T1 OR T2)
C-2	T6 AND (T3 OR T4 OR T5) AND (T1 OR T2) AND T7

Table 3. Search combinations during the second stage of the SLM

ID	Combination
C-1	T6 AND (T3 OR T4 OR T5) AND (T1 OR T2)
C-2	T6 AND (T3 OR T4 OR T5) AND (T1 OR T2) AND (T8 OR T9)

Table 4. Inclusion and exclusion criteria for the SLM

Inclusion Criteria	Any work that responds to one or more of the formulated research questions. Works published either in the English or Spanish languages.
Exclusion Criteria	Works that contain the defined search terms and/or combinations, but do not respond to any of the formulated research questions.

The same review protocol was utilized during both stages of the SLM, which consists of the inclusion and exclusion criteria presented in Table 4.

Realization of the SLM

The process for the search and selection of the publications consisted of the same steps for both stages of the SLM. First, the searches in every bibliographical source for every search combination were realized, obtaining a set of general results. Next, a partial review of the first 200 results per search was realized, which consisted on the reading of mainly the title, abstract and keywords of the publications. For searches that yielded less than 200 results, all of them were reviewed. A set of potentially useful publications was obtained from the partial review, which were then reviewed in-depth, obtaining a final set consisting of the useful publications for the SLM. Table 5 presents the number of publications for both stages of the SLM during every step of the process, as well as the intersection and union of results between both stages. It must be mentioned that, since only the first 200 results of each search have been reviewed, the intersection and union of the general results, which correspond to all the obtained results for each search, cannot be provided.

In this manner, a total of 58 publications have been selected. Three of these publications have been identified both in the first and second stages of the SLM, as it can be observed in Figure 2. A document containing the references to all of the selected publications can be found in: http://colvin.chillan.ubiobio.cl/mcaro/gallegos/ea-adoption/.

Table 5. Results of the SLM

SLM Stage	General Results	Reviewed Publications	Potentially Useful Publications	Selected Publications
Stage 1 (S1)	1,615	435	59	48
Stage 2 (S2)	724	540	17	13
S1 ∩ S2	-	19	4	3
S1 ∪ S2	-	956	72	58

Enterprise Architectures in the Local E-Government Context 51

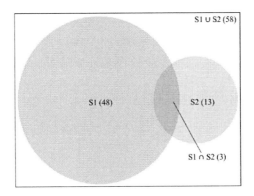

Figure 2. Selected publications during both stages of the SLM.

PRESENTATION AND ANALYSIS OF THE RESULTS

The main findings from the analysis of the results of this SLM are presented in this section. It must be mentioned that, although the study aimed to identify publications that focused on the use of EA in local e-government, part of the accepted publications focused mainly on the use of EA for central e-government. This is because while performing the SLM, it was observed that there was a low number of publications focusing only on EA usage in local e-governments. Figure 3 shows the publications grouped by the kind of focused organization. 58.6% of the publications focused on central e-government, whereas the remaining 41.4% focused on local e-government.

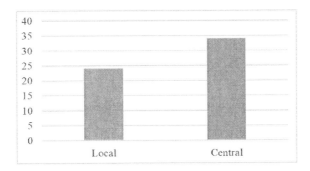

Figure 3. Focus of the EA studies.

Through the rest of this section, both sets of publications will be analyzed as a whole and also separately, as specified for each case.

Years Covered by the Research

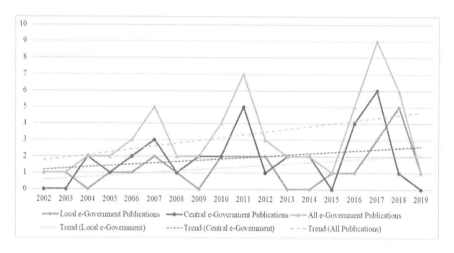

Figure 4. EA in e-government publications per year.

The selected publications range from year 2002 to the present. In general, the interest of the community for tackling the topic of using enterprise architectures in e-government is highlighted. This is evidenced by the increasing trend of publications per year. In Figure 4, the number of selected publications per year, as well as the trend, are shown. It can be seen that, during 2011, there was a rise in the number of publications, which saw a reduction in the upcoming years until 2016, where it had a significant rise again.

The year 2018 is highlighted as it has been the year with the most local e-government publications, whereas only one publication addressed central e-government.

Types of Documents about EA

Regarding the types of publications that were found, most of them correspond to conference articles (14 for local e-government and 17 for central e-government), followed by journal articles (3 for local e-Government and 11 for central e-government), theses (6 for local e-government and 3 for central e-government) and book chapters (1 for local e-government and 3 for central e-government).

Although conferences have received a similar amount of EA-related research for both local and central e-government, it can be observed that thesis works favor researching local e-government, whereas journal articles and book chapters have a higher trend towards central e-government.

Use of Modeling Notations

Table 6. Use of modeling notations in EA publications

Reference	BPMN	Use Case	Archi-Mate	Other Diagrams
EA in Local e-Government Publications				
(Tanaka, de Barros, and de Souza Mendes 2018)			x	
(Setiawan and Yulianto 2018)	x	x		
(Helfert, Melo, and Pourzolfaghar 2018)			x	
(Girón et al. 2018)	x	x		
(Bach. Baez Medina, 2017)	x			
(Jiménez Álvarez 2016)	x			
(Rodríguez Ortiz 2012)	x	x		x
(Koning, Bos, and Brinkkemper 2008)				x
(Lankhorst and Derks 2007)			x	
(Zuiderhoek et al. 2006)				x
EA in Central e-Government Publications				
(Syynimaa 2016)	x		x	
(Aguilar Lugo et al. 2016)	x			
(Gallardo Salas 2011)	x			
(Bouwman et al. 2011)			x	

Regarding the use of EA modeling notations, it can be observed in Table 6 that only 14 publications (24.1%) utilize some notation for describing aspects of the EA. Among these, BPMN is the most used modeling notation. It is highlighted that most of these publications belong to EA in local e-government research, having only a handful of central e-government ones that did specify a modeling notation.

Use of EA Frameworks

Figure 5 shows the analyzed publications in relation to the frameworks that have been utilized for the creation of the distinct enterprise architectures. Additionally, Table 7 presents the number of publications per year that mention their utilized framework. For example, in 2017, TOGAF and the Colombian Reference Framework were used in one publication each for local e-government, whereas TOGAF was used twice, and GEA, Zachman and another framework were used once each for central e-government. The most used framework is TOGAF, as 17.2% of the publications have used it. It must be mentioned that 26 (44.8%) of the publications did not specify the framework that was used for the creation of the proposed EA.

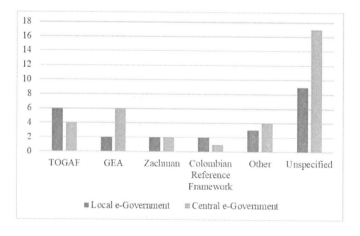

Figure 5. Use of frameworks in EA publications.

Enterprise Architectures in the Local E-Government Context 55

Table 7. Frameworks used in EA publications per year

Year	Local	Central
2004	-	Other (1)
2005	-	GEA (1)
2006	Other (1)	-
2007	Zachman (1)	-
2008	Other (1)	-
2009	-	GEA (2)
2010	GEA (1)	GEA (1)
2011	GEA (1), Other (1)	TOGAF (1), Other (1)
2012	Zachman (1)	Zachman (1)
2013	-	GEA (1)
2014	-	-
2015	-	-
2016	Colombian Reference Framework (1)	TOGAF (1), Colombian Reference Framework (1)
2017	TOGAF (1), Colombian Reference Framework (1)	TOGAF (2), GEA (1), Zachman (1), Other (1)
2018	TOGAF (5)	Other (1)

EA Dimensions Considered by the Publications

Table 8. Dimensions considered in EA implementations

Dimension	Local e-Government Publications	Central e-Government Publications
Strategy	1	0
Business	3	3
Information Systems (Application and Data)	2	0
Business and Information Systems	4	1
Information Systems and Technology	0	1
Strategy, Business and Information Systems	0	1
Strategy, Information Systems and Technology	0	1
Business, Information Systems and Technology	5	5

The realization of the SLM allowed to observe that not all publications considered the implementation of all the dimensions that can be modeled in an EA. Moreover, this is also dependent on the EA framework that is being utilized, as some of them may consider dimensions that are not considered in others. The dimensions that have been identified in the distinct publications have been analyzed and normalized, as shown in Table 8. A total of 15 local e-government and 12 central e-government publications indicated the dimensions that were implemented in their EA.

Classification of EA Publications by Country

The country to which every publication belonged was identified, as seen in Table 9. To facilitate the analysis, the countries were then grouped based on their geographical region, as shown in Figure 6. It can be observed that most publications regarding enterprise architectures in e-government are from Europe, followed by the Ibero-America and the Caribbean, and the Pacific and Far East regions. Conversely, only one publication from North America was found.

Table 9. Publications about EA in e-government by country

Country	Local	Central	Sum	Country	Local	Central	Sum
Finland	4	5	9	Iran	0	1	1
Holland	5	3	8	Italy	0	1	1
Indonesia	2	2	4	Mexico	1	0	1
Peru	2	2	4	Norway	0	1	1
Colombia	2	1	3	Palestine	1	0	1
Australia	0	2	2	South Africa	0	1	1
Sweden	2	0	2	South Korea	0	1	1
Brazil	1	0	1	Tunisia	0	1	1
Denmark	0	1	1	United Kingdom	0	1	1
Greece	1	0	1	Multiple Countries	1	5	6
Ireland	1	0	1	Global	1	5	6
Hungary	0	1	1				

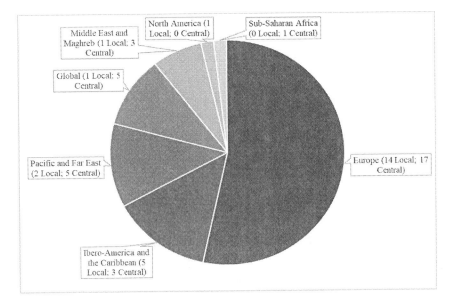

Figure 6. Publications about EA in e-government by geographical region.

A certain trend towards the use of EA for local e-government can be observed among the publications from Latin American countries.

DISCUSSION

The main findings of the SLM are discussed in this section. This is done by providing answers to every posed research question.

Adoption Level of EA in Local e-Government (Q1)

It is important to highlight that the use of EA in e-government has been increasing throughout the years, which is evidenced by an increasing trend of publications. However, it must be mentioned that only 41.4% of the identified publications address local e-government, whereas the remainder focus on central e-government. A possible explanation for this could be that many municipalities lack the necessary economical, time and human resources for attempting to implement an EA on their own (Plummer 2013; Cruz Bueno and Briceño Pineda 2014). Another possible explanation lies in the lack of knowledge from the municipality's workforce regarding EA. For an adequate modeling, it is required that the involved personnel must already have experience in the development of an EA. Moreover, it is essential to understand how the organization's strategy and motivational aspects relate with the functioning of its business processes, information systems and data for them to appropriately implement an EA (Cruz Bueno and Briceño Pineda 2014; Jiménez Álvarez 2016; The Open Group 2017).

A varied adoption level of EA can be observed in the reviewed publications, as not all of them considered the implementation of all the basic dimensions that should be included in an EA. Only 37% of the publications that indicated the implemented dimensions have included all three main dimensions (business, information systems and technology).

It can be observed that governmental institutions highly value the importance of the business dimension, as it is present in 81.5% of the publications that indicated the implemented dimensions.

When considering only EA in local e-government publications, the above numbers are slightly lower, with 33.4% of the publications including all three main dimensions, and 80% of the municipalities implementing the business dimension.

Regions of the World that use EA for Local e-Government (Q2)

It can be seen that most of the research on EA both in the context of local e-government and of central e-government has been performed in Europe, especially in Finland and Holland. The former has focused on central e-government slightly more, whereas the latter has focused on local e-government slightly more. A considerable number of publications belonging to the Ibero-America and the Caribbean, and the Pacific and Far East regions have also been found. However, publications from other countries that are known for their use of EA in e-government, such as the United States (Guijarro 2007), were not found during this research. A possible explanation for this could be that, although the central governments of these countries utilize EA, their implementation at a local level has been done to a lower degree or has not been documented in literature.

Frameworks Used for EA in Local e-Government (Q3)

Various frameworks have been used for the creation of EA in e-government. The two most used ones have been TOGAF and GEA. However, it is important to observe the publication years of the works that use these frameworks: publications utilizing GEA are generally older, whereas those that use TOGAF are from recent years. This can be explained as, throughout time, TOGAF has become the standard for EA modeling (The Open Group 2011).

In addition to the above, TOGAF has also been used more often in local e-government implementations of EA, whereas GEA has been used more often in central e-government.

Nevertheless, it must also be mentioned that nearly half of the publications did not specifically mention what framework was utilized for the creation of the EA.

Notations Used for EA in Local e-Government (Q4)

A lack on the usage of modeling notations for the creation of EA in the context of e-government can be seen. Only a fourth of the studies utilize notations. However, when considering only the studies that focus on local e-government, the percentage of publications that use modeling notations rises to 41.7%. On the other hand, only 11.8% of the publications focusing on central e-government used modeling notations.

BPMN is the most used modeling notation, followed by use case diagrams and ArchiMate. The fact that BPMN is used the most could be due to the importance that was observed to be given to the business layer by the organizations, as BPMN is the standard for modeling processes in the business dimension (Chinosi and Trombetta 2012).

CONCLUSION

The results of a Systematic Literature Mapping that had the objective of identifying the bibliographic material that allows understanding the use and adoption levels of Enterprise Architectures in the context of local e-government have been provided in this chapter. A total of 58 publications that help to address the topic have been identified.

The results allow to obtain a number of conclusions. First of all, a low level of adoption in the use of EA in local e-governments can be observed, as more than half of the identified publications do not address the use of EA directly in municipalities, but rather focusing on central government. Additionally, a considerable number of the publications did not consider the implementation of a complete EA, but rather of some of its dimensions, being the business dimension the most observed.

Secondly, Europe is highlighted as the region with the most advancements in EA adoption for e-government, as more than half of the identified publications provide studies in this region.

Thirdly, although GEA and the Zachman framework had been favored previously, a trend in the use of TOGAF as the framework for modeling EA in local e-government can be seen in recent years.

Finally, the need for a greater use of notations in EA modeling is emphasized, as only 5 of the identified publications used ArchiMate, which is a dedicated EA modeling language. Other publications mentioned the use of complementary notations like BPMN and use case diagrams, which help to model some of the features of an EA mainly in the business layer, but most publications did not indicate the use of any notation.

The results and the analysis provided in this SLM aim to serve as a starting point both for academia and governmental agents interested in further researching or implementing EA in e-government.

Among the future work that is considered for this research, the implementation of a standardized EA for local governments is highlighted. This EA would have a focus on the provision of services to the citizenship, as this is one of the main goals of a municipality. Moreover, it is of interest to define an adoption methodology that allows to solve the current barriers for the implementation of EA in a local level, such as the lack of economic, time and human resources by the municipality, or of the necessary knowledge on EA by its workforce.

REFERENCES

Aguilar Lugo, Karina Yuliana, Alex Martín Díaz Cruz, Llanos Sánchez, and Alexander Michael. 2016. *Propuesta de modelo de arquitectura de negocio usando un marco de arquitectura empresarial para una entidad pública.* [Business enterprise model proposal using an enterprise architecture framework for a public entity.]

Ask, Andreas, and Karin Hedström. 2011. "Taking initial steps towards enterprise architecture in local government." *International Conference on Electronic Government and the Information Systems Perspective.*

Batlle Montserrat, Joan, Ernest Abadal, and Josep Blat. 2011. "Benchmarking del e-gobierno local: limitaciones de los sistemas de evaluación comparativa." *El Profesional de la Informacion, 2011, vol. 20, num. 3, p. 251-259.* ["Benchmarking of local e-government: limitations of comparative evaluation systems." *The Information Professional, 2011, vol. 20, num. 3, p. 251-259.*]

Bouwman, Harry, Harrie van Houtum, Marijn Janssen, and Gerrit Versteeg. 2011. "Business architectures in the public sector: experiences from practice." *Communications of the Association for Information Systems* 29 (1): 23.

Carter, Lemuria, and France Bélanger. 2005. "The utilization of e-government services: citizen trust, innovation and acceptance factors." *Information systems journal* 15 (1): 5-25.

Chinosi, Michele, and Alberto Trombetta. 2012. "BPMN: An introduction to the standard." *Computer Standards & Interfaces* 34 (1): 124-134.

Cruz Bueno, Hernán Darío, and Wilson Briceño Pineda. 2014. "Factores Relevantes para Inicio de Arquitecturas Empresariales en el Sector Público Colombiano. Estudio Bibliométrico." *Revista GTI* 13 (35): 63-77. ["Relevant Factors for Starting Enterprise Architectures in the Colombian Public Sector. Bibliometric Study." *GTI Journal* 13 (35): 63-77.]

Duszak, Anna, and Jo Lewkowicz. 2008. "Publishing academic texts in English: A Polish perspective." *Journal of English for Academic Purposes* 7 (2): 108-120.

Gallardo Salas, Herbert Joseth. 2011. *Mejora de servicios de una entidad del estado utilizando Six Sigma y arquitectura empresarial. Caso: Servicio de pensionamiento ONP.* [*Improvement of services of a state entity using Six Sigma and enterprise architecture. Case: ONP pensions service.*]

Gallegos-Baeza, Daniela, Ignacio Velásquez, Alfonso Rodríguez, and Angélica Caro. 2019. "Uso de Arquitecturas Empresariales en e-Government Municipal: Un Mapeo Sistemático de la Literatura." *Revista Ibérica de Sistemas e Tecnologias de Informação* (E17): 816-829. ["Use of Enterprise Architectures in Municipal e-Government: A Systematic Mapping of Literature." *Iberican Journal of Information Systems and Technologies* (E17): 816-829.]

Genero Bocco, Marcela, José Cruz Lemus, and Mario Piattini Velthuis. 2014. *Métodos de investigación en ingeniería del software.* Ra-Ma Editorial. [*Research methods in software engineering.* Ra-Ma Editorial.]

Girón, García, Allison Janisse, Hinostroza Lozada, and Raphel Xavier. 2018. *Modelo de mejoras de e-servicios municipales.* [*Municipal e-services improvements model.*]

Grossi, Giuseppe, and Christoph Reichard. 2016. "Variance in the institutions of local utility services: Evidence from several European countries." In *Public and Social Services in Europe*, 297-312. Springer.

Guijarro, Luis. 2007. "Interoperability frameworks and enterprise architectures in e-government initiatives in Europe and the United States." *Government Information Quarterly* 24 (1): 89-101.

Helfert, Markus, Viviana Angely Bastidas Melo, and Zohreh Pourzolfaghar. 2018. "Digital and Smart Services-The Application of Enterprise Architecture." *International Conference on Digital Transformation and Global Society*.

Hornnes, Erik, Arild Jansen, and Øivind Langeland. 2010. "How to develop an open and flexible information infrastructure for the public sector?" *International Conference on Electronic Government*.

Jiménez Álvarez, Jhon Jairo. 2016. *Modelo para la creación de secretaría tic en entes territoriales colombianos de categoría 1 y 2, basado en arquitectura empresarial.* [Model for the creation of ict secretariat in territorial Colombian entities of category 1 and 2, based on enterprise architecture.]

Kitchenham, Barbara, Pearl Brereton, David Budgen, Mark Turner, John Bailey, and Stephen Linkman. 2009. "Systematic literature reviews in software engineering–a systematic literature review." *Information and software technology* 51 (1): 7-15.

Koning, Henk, Rik Bos, and Sjaak Brinkkemper. 2008. "A lightweight method for the modelling of enterprise architectures." *International Conference on Service-Oriented Computing*.

Lankhorst, Marc, and Wijnand Derks. 2007. "Towards A Service-Oriented Architecture for Demand-Driven e Government." *11th IEEE International Enterprise Distributed Object Computing Conference (EDOC 2007)*.

Lankhorst, Marc, Henderik Alex Proper, and Henk Jonkers. 2010. "The anatomy of the archimate language." *International Journal of Information System Modeling and Design (IJISMD)* 1 (1): 1-32.

Moon, Jae. 2002. "The evolution of e-government among municipalities: rhetoric or reality?" *Public administration review* 62 (4): 424-433.

Navarro, Celia Chaín, Antonio Muñoz Cañavate, and Amalia Más Bleda. 2008. "La gestión de información en las sedes web de los ayuntamientos españoles." *Revista española de documentación científica* 31 (4): 612-638. ["Information management in the web sites of Spanish municipalities." *Spanish journal of scientific documentation* 31 (4): 612-638.]

Paiva Dias, Gonçalo. 2011. "Local e-government information and service delivery." *6th Iberian Conference on Information Systems and Technologies* (CISTI 2011).

Petersen, Kai, Sairam Vakkalanka, and Ludwik Kuzniarz. 2015. "Guidelines for conducting systematic mapping studies in software engineering: An update." *Information and Software Technology* 64: 1-18.

Plummer, Janelle. 2013. *Municipalities and community participation: a sourcebook for capacity building.* Routledge.

Poggi, Eduardo. 2013. "Gobierno electrónico, gobierno local y gestión tecnológica." Pando, D. y Fernández Arroyo, N. (comp.), *El gobierno electrónico a nivel local. Experiencias, tendencias y reflexiones*: 71-95. ["Electronic government, local government and technological management." Pando, D. and Fernández Arroyo, N. (comp.), *Electronic government at a local level. Experiences, tendencies and reflections*: 71-95.]

Rodríguez Ortiz, Iván. 2012. "Infraestructura Tecnológica y Sistemas de Información para la Oferta de Servicios de Gobierno Electrónico a Nivel Municipal." [*"Technological Infrastructure and Information Systems for Offering Electronic Government Services at a Municipal Level."*]

Sandoval Almazan, Rodrigo, and Jeanett Mendoza Colin. 2011. "Gobierno electrónico en México: Una exploración municipal 2010." *17th Americas Conference on Information Systems 2011,* AMCIS 2011. ["Electronic government in Mexico: A municipal exploration 2010." *17th Americas Conference on Information Systems 2011,* AMCIS 2011.]

Setiawan, Awan, and Erwin Yulianto. 2018. "E-Government Interoperability and Integration Architecture Modeling Using TOGAF Framework Based On Service Oriented Architecture." *The Asian Journal of Technology Management* 11 (1): 26-45.

Syynimaa, Nestori. 2016. "Method and Practical Guidelines for Overcoming Enterprise Architecture Adoption Challenges." *International Conference on Enterprise Information Systems.*

Tanaka, Sergio Akio, Rodolfo Miranda de Barros, and Leonardo de Souza Mendes. 2018. "A Proposal to a Framework for Governance of ICT Aiming At Smart Cities with a Focus on Enterprise Architecture." *Proceedings of the XIV Brazilian Symposium on Information Systems.*

The Open Group. 2011. *TOGAF specification.* Version 9.1.

The Open Group. 2017. *ArchiMate ® 3.0.1 Specification.*

Vakkala, Hanna, and Jaana Leinonen. 2020. "Current Features and Developments of Local Governance in Finland: The Changing Roles of Citizens and Municipalities." In *Open Government: Concepts, Methodologies, Tools, and Applications*, 1849-1872. IGI Global.

Zachman, John. 1996. *Concepts of the framework for enterprise architecture.* Los Angeles.

Zuiderhoek, Bastiaan, Arjan Otter, Rik Bos, and Sjaak Brinkkemper. 2006. "Framework for Dutch municipalities to ensure business IT alignment using enterprise architecture." *Proceedings of the 6th European Conference on e-Government.*

In: E-Government
Editor: Anil Sieben

ISBN: 978-1-53617-563-9
© 2020 Nova Science Publishers, Inc.

Chapter 3

EMPIRICAL EVALUATION OF E-GOVERNMENT USING A COMBINATION OF DECISION MAKING METHODS

Katerina Kabassi[*]
Department of Environment, Ionian University,
Zakynthos, Greece

ABSTRACT

The significant investments made by governments around the world in developing e-government capabilities make it essential to evaluate them systemically; if they are to improve the value they generate (Sterrenberg 2017). One of the critical issues for both researchers and the governments is how to evaluate and assess the value of such projects (Liu & Wang 2008). Therefore, Kunstelj & Vintar (2004) focus on the need for evaluating e-Government and express the need for improved methods of evaluation. As a result, evaluation of e-government implementation has attracted the attention of researchers within the last two decades and some research work in this domain has been conducted evaluating government websites (Kaaya 2001; Kaylor et al. 2002; Boussarhan and

---
[*] Corresponding Author's E-mail: kkabassi@ionio.gr.

Daoudi 2014, Oni et al. 2016). However, as Sterrenberg (2017) points out, past studies that involve evaluating e-government have been somewhat limited, despite the fact that e-government has had an important impact on the way public services have been delivered in recent years. In view of the above and in an effort to present a well-established evaluation experiment of e-Government, we present an empirical evaluation that combines two different Multi-Criteria Decision Making Techniques, called AHP and TOPSIS. The paper summarizes and presents the steps that need to be taken for the application of these theories in comparing e-government sites based on criteria that have been collected using the outcome of the literature review of AHP evaluation studies of e-Government. The evaluation experiment compares five sites for e-government in Greece with the participation of 78 real users. Greece was selected as it is a country that tries hard the latter years to improve the way the government services are performed and improve e-government.

Keywords: e-government, evaluation, AHP

1. INTRODUCTION

The focus of e-government is on the provision of governmental services via the use of information technology with the aim of enhancing the service level relationships between government and its various stakeholder groups, such as the citizen, businesses, tourists and other governmental agencies (UN, 2008). The significant investments made by governments around the world in developing e-government capabilities make it essential to evaluate them systemically if they are to improve the value they generate (Sterrenberg 2017).

Kunstelj & Vintar (2004) focus on the need for evaluating e-Government and express the need for improved methods of evaluation. One of the critical issues for both researchers and governments is how to evaluate and assess the value of such projects (Liu & Wang 2008). Therefore, the evaluation of e-government implementation has attracted the attention of researchers within the last two decades. Some research work in this domain has been conducted using government websites (Kaaya 2001; Kaylor et al. 2002; Boussarhan and Daoudi 2014, Oni et al.

2016). However, as Sterrenberg (2017) points out, past studies of evaluating e-government have been somewhat limited, despite the fact that e-government has had an important impact on the way public services have been delivered in recent years.

For the evaluation of a website different methods exist. Lewis & Rieman (1994), as well as Davoli et al. (2005), distinguish methods to empirical methods and inspection methods. In inspection methods, the evaluators are experts and, in empirical methods, the evaluators are potential users with different characteristics. Each method has different advantages and disadvantages. For example, expert-based evaluations are easier and cheaper compared to empirical ones (Reeves 1993; Karoulis et al. 2006). Empirical methods, on the other hand, may be more successful in capturing end user's perceptions as real users participate in the experiment (Kabassi 2017). Kabassi (2018) used an inspection method to evaluate five e-Government sites in Greece. In this paper, we evaluated the same e-government sites using an empirical method of evaluation.

The evaluation of an electronic service or a website is a multidimensional problem that depends on several criteria and different aspects of the evaluators. For this purpose, Multi-Criteria Decision Making (MCDM) theories seem rather suitable for software evaluation. As a result, MCDM theories have been used for evaluating different software systems (Kabassi 2009, Kabassi et al. 2011, Kabassi 2018). For example, Kabassi (2018) used Analytic Hierarchy Process (AHP) (Saaty 1980) for structuring an experiment for the evaluation e-Government websites. However, AHP does not seem appropriate if the theory is solely used in empirical evaluations. This is due to the fact that its application requires filling out several tables and makes the procedure really hard to follow for the potential users of the experiment. For this purpose, a new evaluation experiment has been designed to implement an empirical evaluation of e-Government websites.

The evaluation experiment described in this paper makes use of two different Multi Criteria Decision Making (MCDM) theories: AHP (Analytic Hierarchy Process) (Saaty 1980) and TOPSIS (Technique for Order of Preference by Similarity to Ideal Solution) (Hwang & Yoon

1981). AHP aims to analyze a qualitative problem through a quantitative method (Saaty 1980). TOPSIS, on the other hand, aims at ordering evaluation items, which in our case are museum websites, through detecting distance between evaluated objects and optimal solutions (Hwang & Yoon 1981). More specifically, we have used an inspection method in combination with AHP for extracting the weights of the criteria and TOPSIS in combination with the empirical method for comparing the e-Government websites. In order to demonstrate the usefulness of the experiment set in real-world evaluation studies, we conducted an evaluation experiment where we compare five sites for e-government in Greece. Greece was selected as it is a country that tries hard the latter years to improve the way the government services are performed and improve e-government.

The paper is organized as follows: Section 2 describes the application of AHP for setting the set of criteria and calculating their weights. In the next section, TOPSIS is presented in detail for evaluating the different e-government websites. In section 4, the set of the alternative e-government websites are presented and then in the next section, the application of TOPSIS is presented together with the estimations and the results of the evaluation. In the last section of the paper, we discuss the results of the evaluation and present the conclusions drawn by this work.

2. AHP FOR SETTING CRITERIA AND WEIGHTS

AHP was selected amongst other MCDM theories because it presents a formal way of quantifying the qualitative criteria of the alternatives and in this way removes the subjectivity of the result (Tiwari 2006). Furthermore, the method has the ability to making decisions by making pairwise comparisons of uncertain, qualitative and quantitative factors and also can model expert opinion (Mulubrhan et al. 2014). This part of the experiment has also been implemented in an inspection evaluation of e-government websites (Kabassi 2018). However, the inspection experiment described in (Kabassi 2018) differentiates with the empirical evaluation in the next phase of the application of the MCDM theory that is described in the next section.

The method consists of the following steps (Zhu & Buchman 2000):

1. Developing a goal hierarchy. The overall goal, criteria and decision alternatives are arranged in a hierarchical structure.
2. Making pairwise comparisons for calculating the weights of the criteria. This step requires locating the list of criteria and then calculating the weights of these criteria.
3. Comparing e-government websites

We implement the first two steps and then we use a different theory, TOPSIS, to implement the third step. This is due to the fact that after decomposing the problem into a hierarchy, alternatives at a given hierarchy level are compared in pairs to assess their relative preference with regard to each criterion at the higher level. In order to implement this, it is required to complete one 5 x 5 table for each criterion of the evaluation for making pairwise comparisons of the e-Government websites. This approach may be effective for an inspection evaluation experiment where the evaluators are experts but do not seem appropriate for empirical evaluation experiment in which the evaluators are potential users of the system because it requires a lot of effort from the participants of the experiment.

In this phase of AHP, the overall goal, criteria and decision alternatives are arranged in a hierarchical structure. For this purpose, the following steps are implemented:

1. *Forming the overall goal:* The overall goal is the evaluation of e-government by real users.
2. *Forming the set of criteria:* In order to locate the criteria that are going to be used for the evaluation of the e-Government criteria, we reviewed some of the evaluation experiments on e-government that used the AHP theory (Kabassi 2018). For this purpose, twelve evaluation experiments of e-government sites that use AHP (Tongnoy et al. 2012, Dominic & Jati 2010, Byun & Finnie 2011,

Liu et al. 2010, Liu & Wang 2008, Zhu et al. 2007, Papadomichelaki et al. 2013), fuzzy AHP or their combination with other methods in e-government evaluation were examined (Büyüközkan & Ruan 2007, Zhu & Liu 2011, Yao et al. 2010, Burmaoglu & Kazancoglu 2012, Wang 2010). This process resulted in the criteria presented in Table 1.

3. *Calculating the weights of the criteria:* In this phase of AHP, all the essential pairwise comparisons of the criteria are made in order to calculate the weights of the criteria. The decision-makers are the expert users on the field and a correct choice of the experts would give reliable and valid results (Kabassi 2018). In this example, 5 different civil servants participated in a group of decision-makers. The decision-makers were asked to participate in all steps of the application of AHP in the evaluation of the criteria as well as the e-government websites that were evaluated. For this purpose, the following steps are implemented:

- *Setting up a pairwise comparison matrix of criteria:* In this step, a comparison matrix is built and the comparison is implemented among the criteria of the same level. In the comparison process, a V from the scale is assigned to the comparison result of two elements P and Q at first, then the value of comparison of Q and P is a reciprocal value of V, i.e., 1/V. The value of the comparison between P and P is 1. For example, if the evaluation experiment has two levels of criteria (e.g., Jadhav & Sonar 2011, Mohamadali & Garibaldi 2011) the criteria of each level are compared separately. This process results in the creation of a matrix for the comparison of the criteria of the first level and three matrixes for comparing the criteria of the second level. As we have 5 different civil servants, 5 such matrixes are created. Each cell of the final matrix is calculated as the integer which is closer to the geometric mean of the five matrixes collected by the decision-makers. Experts use the nine scale of Saaty (1980) to represent the varying degrees of preference.

- *Calculating* weights of criteria: After making pairwise comparisons, estimations are made that result in the final set of weights of the criteria. In terms of simplicity, we have use the 'Priority Estimation Tool' (PriEst) (Sirah et al. 2015), an open-source decision-making software that implements the AHP method, for making the calculations of AHP. This process is analysed in more details in Kabassi (2018). The weights that were calculated through this process are: wContent and appearance = 0.058, wReliability = 0.645, wSystem/Service quality = 0.297, wInformation quality = 0.192, wNavigability = 0.186, wGraphic design/User Interface = 0.09, wUser care = 0.08, wFAQs and help = 0.54, wCitizen support = 0.123, wSatisfaction/Enjoyment = 0.052, wEase of use/Usability = 0.224, wSecurity = 0.667, w =, wPrivacy = 0.333, wLoad time = 0.137, wResponsiveness/speed=0.141, wExternal recognition = 0.036, wLinks = 0.050, wPersonalisation = 0.114, wRelevancy = 0.087, wCurrency/accuracy/validation = 0.224, wFunctionality/technology = 0.074, wWebServices = 0.059, wInteraction/Participation = 0.41, wRichness/attractiveness = 0.037.

3. TOPSIS: Comparing E-Government Websites

After having calculated the weights of the criteria, the e-government websites are compared. For this purpose, a group of 78 real potential users of the e-Government website was formed. The users of this group should have different characteristics, having different interests and background knowledge. The correct choice of the users participating in this group of evaluators ensures the success of evaluation experiment.

Table 1. Criteria for evaluating e-government websites using AHP (Kabassi 2018)

	Tongnoy et al. 2012	Dominic et al. 2010	Papadomichelaki et al. 2013	Büyüközkan and Ruan 2007	Byun & Finnie (2011)	Zhu & Liu 2011	Yao et al. 2010	Burmaoglu & Kazancoglu 2012	Liu et al. 2010	Liu & Wang 2008	Zhu et al. 2007	Wang 2010
Content and appearance	1			1	1	1	1		1		1	
Ca1: Information quality			2	1		1	1			1	2	2
Ca2: Navigability			2	2	1			2		2		
Ca3: Graphic design/User Interface			2	2	2		2			2	2	
Ca4: User care			2	2			2					
Ca5: FAQs and help			2	2	2			2	2	2		2
Ca6: Citizen support (interactivity)			2	1	2		2			2		
Ca7: Satisfaction/Enjoyment					2		1	2				
Ca8: Ease of use/Usability					2		1			2		2
Reliability			1	1			1				2	
Re1: Security			2	2	2			2	2	2	2	2
Re2: Privacy			2	2	2				2	2	2	2

System/Service quality	Tongnoy et al. 2012	Dominic et al. 2010	Papadomichelaki et al. 2013	Büyüközkan and Ruan 2007	Byun & Finnie (2011)	Zhu & Liu 2011	Yao et al. 2010	Burmaoglu & Kazancoglu 2012	Liu et al. 2010	Liu & Wang 2008	Zhu et al. 2007	Wang 2010
Ss1: Load time	1	1	2		2					2	2	2
Ss2: Responsiveness/speed		1	2	1	2					2	2	
Ss3: External recognition			2	2								
Ss4: Links		1	2		2		2	2	2	2	2	
Ss5: Personalisation			2	2	2			2	2		2	
Ss6: Relevancy			2	2				2				
Ss7: Currency/accuracy/validation		1	2	2	2	1	2	2	2	2		
Ss8: Functionality/technology									2	1		
Ss9: WebServices					2	1	2	1	2	1	2	2
Ss10: Interaction/Participation							1	2	2	2	2	
Ss11: Richness/attractiveness								2		2		

1. *Calculating the values of the criteria:* Each one of the users participating in the experiment was asked to visit all e-Government websites that were evaluated in the experiment that they participate. Then focusing on each one of the e-Government websites each user was asked to give a value to each one of the 22 criteria presented in Table 1. The values given for each criterion by the evaluators must be taken from the nine-number AHP scale (Table 2) so the values can be comparable.

Table 2. Evaluation scale for criteria/alternatives

Importance	Definition	Explanation
1	Equal importance	The importance of the two criteria or alternatives is equal
2	Weak	
3	Moderate importance	A slight favor of one criterion or alternative over another
4	Moderate plus	
5	Strong importance	A strong favor of one criterion or alternative over another
6	Strong plus	
7	Very strong importance	A very strong favor of one criterion or alternative over another
8	Very, very strong	
9	Extreme importance	One criterion or alternative is surely favored over another

1. *Calculate weighted ratings.* The weighted value is calculated as $v_{ij} = w_i \cdot r_{ij}$, where w_i is the weight and r_{ij} is the value of the ith criterion.
2. *Identify positive-ideal and negative-ideal alternative.* The positive-ideal solution is the composite of all the best attribute ratings attainable, and it is denoted as $A^* = \{v_1^*, v_2^*, ..., v_i^*, ..., v_n^*\}$, where v_i^* is the best value for the ith attribute among all alternatives. The negative-ideal solution is the composite of all the worst attribute

ratings attainable, and it is denoted as $A^- = \{v_1^-, v_2^-, ..., v_i^-, ..., v_n^-\}$, where v_i^- is the worst value for the ith attribute among all alternatives.

3. *Calculate the separation measure from the positive-ideal and negative-ideal alternatives.* The separation of each alternative from the positive-ideal solution, A^*, is given by the n-dimensional Euclidean distance $S_j^* = \sqrt{\sum_{i=1}^{n}(v_{ij} - v_i^*)^2}$, where j is the index related to the alternatives and i is each one of the n criteria. Similarly, the separation from the negative-ideal solution A^- is given by $S_j^- = \sqrt{\sum_{i=1}^{n}(v_{ij} - v_i^-)^2}$.

4. *Calculate similarity indices.* The similarity to the positive-ideal solution for alternative j is finally given by $C_j^* = \dfrac{S_j^-}{S_j^* + S_j^-}$, with $0 \leq C_j^* \leq 1$. The alternatives can then be ranked according to C_j^* in descending order.

5. *Ranking e-Government websites.* The similarity indices are further used to rank the e-Government websites that are evaluated, and the one with the higher value is selected as the best.

4. FINDING E-GOVERNMENT WEBSITES

In this step, the final set of alternative websites is formed. In this paper, we present the evaluation experiment of the same five popular e-Government websites in Greece that were also evaluated in (Kabassi 2018). However, the process of evaluation is quite different from the one described in (Kabassi 2018), in which the experts that participated in the inspection evaluation had to make pairwise comparisons of the websites. In this experiment, the evaluators, which are real potential users of the e-government websites, had to evaluate each website separately and provide values to the criteria, without taking into account the other alternatives.

- OPT-1: EFKA (http://www.efka.gov.gr). EFKA is the largest Social Security Organization in Greece. EFKA covers the independent employment in Greece or abroad for an employer who is based in Greece, as well as those who offer full-time or part-time personal labor on commissioned work agreements and are not insured with any other Main Insurance agency. The website contains only general information in English although there are many foreigners working in Greece.
- OPT-2: ERMIS (http://www.ermis.gov.gr/). The website provides access to several e-services that can normally be completed by a KEP (Citizens' Service Center). The interface is user-friendly and what is really impressive is that it provides information and access to e-services in 4 languages.
- OPT-3: GSIS (http://www.gsis.gr/). GSIS is the official website of the Greek Ministry of Finance and gives access to several e-services. The interface is generally friendly and can be used by intermediate users (not novices). It does not provide information in other languages. Although the 'Sign In' web page is in English, when someone is signed in s/he is given information in Greek.
- OPT-4: DEI (https://www.dei.gr/el). DEI is the Greek Electricity Corporation and through the website, the user can have access to e-services that are connected to the bill and general information about the programs and the corporation. It provides all the information and e-services in English and Greek.
- OPT-5: GEODATA (http://geodata.gov.gr/). GEODATA is the Greek government's first attempt to aggregate all geospatial data managed by various public agencies and provide them free of charge through the internet. The interface is simple and easy to use and can be effectively used to search and download various thematic layers categorized by type and responsible agency. The

data are provided in different formats (shapefile, GML, KML) and through a map viewer the data can be viewed before they are downloaded.

5. IMPLEMENTATION OF THE EVALUATION EXPERIMENT

The 78 potential users of the e-government website that participated in the experiment were asked to visit the five selected e-Government websites. Focusing on each one of the e-Government websites, they were asked to give a value to each one of the 22 criteria. Then the mean of all values was calculated for each criterion. Then, the weighted values of the criteria are calculated taking into account the values of the criteria that were estimated using the AHP theory (Table 3).

As soon as all the weighted values of the criteria are estimated the positive-ideal and negative-ideal alternative should be identified. The positive-ideal solution A^* is the composite of all the best attribute ratings attainable, and are presented in the 7th column of Table 3. Correspondingly, the negative-ideal solution A^- is the composite of all the worst attribute ratings attainable, which are presented in the 8th column of Table 3.

The main idea of TOPSIS is to calculate how far each alternative is from the fictional positive-ideal solution A^* and the fictional negative-ideal solution A^-. For this purpose, the separation measure from the positive-ideal and negative-ideal alternative are calculated using the n-dimensional Euclidean distance $S_j^* = \sqrt{\sum_{i=1}^{22}(v_{ij} - v_i^*)^2}$, where j is the index related to the alternatives and i is each one of the 22 criteria. Similarly, the separation from the negative-ideal solution A^- is given by $S_j^- = \sqrt{\sum_{i=1}^{22}(v_{ij} - v_i^-)^2}$ (Table 4). Those values are used for the calculation of the similarity to the positive-ideal solution for each one of the 5 alternatives (Table 5). The alternatives can then be ranked according to C_j^* in descending order. The final ranking is presented in the last column of Table 5.

The results showed the website of GSIS was considered to be the best related to all the others. However, the similarity indices to the ideal alternative of the websites of ERMIS-KEP and DEI did not have a big difference from the first one, and, therefore, considered almost equally good. Then was the website of GEODATA which had different services but most of the users participating the experiment had not used it before contrary to the websites ranked among the top three.

Table 3. The weighted values of the criteria assigned by the users

	EFKA	ERMIS	GSIS	DEI	GEODATA	v_i^*	v_i^-
Ca1	0,94	1,15	1,15	1,15	1,34	1,34	0,94
Ca2	1,11	1,31	1,31	1,31	1,31	1,31	1,11
Ca3	0,44	0,56	0,53	0,56	0,57	0,57	0,44
Ca4	0,24	0,57	0,57	0,57	0,37	0,57	0,24
Ca5	1,64	3,82	3,82	3,82	1,64	3,82	1,64
Ca6	0,60	0,73	0,73	0,67	0,73	0,73	0,60
Ca7	0,25	0,31	0,30	0,31	0,31	0,31	0,25
Ca8	1,10	1,66	1,55	1,66	1,77	1,77	1,10
Re1	4,45	4,45	4,71	4,45	4,71	4,71	4,45
Re2	2,22	2,22	2,35	2,22	2,35	2,35	2,22
Ss1	0,95	0,97	0,95	0,97	0,97	0,97	0,95
Ss2	0,98	1,00	0,98	1,00	1,00	1,00	0,98
Ss3	0,21	0,21	0,21	0,21	0,21	0,21	0,21
Ss4	0,30	0,32	0,32	0,30	0,20	0,32	0,20
Ss5	0,25	0,45	0,45	0,45	0,25	0,45	0,25
Ss6	0,52	0,52	0,52	0,52	0,52	0,52	0,52
Ss7	1,34	1,34	1,34	1,34	1,34	1,34	1,34
Ss8	0,44	0,44	0,44	0,44	0,44	0,44	0,44
Ss9	0,35	0,38	0,38	0,35	0,35	0,38	0,35
Ss10	2,01	2,17	2,17	2,01	2,01	2,17	2,01
Ss11	0,18	0,23	0,23	0,18	0,26	0,26	0,18

Table 4. The separation measures from the positive-ideal and negative-ideal alternative

S^*_{opt-1}	2,39	S^-_{opt-1}	0,10
S^*_{opt-2}	0,37	S^-_{opt-2}	2,32
S^*_{opt-3}	0,30	S^-_{opt-3}	2,31
S^*_{opt-4}	0,42	S^-_{opt-4}	2,31
S^*_{opt-5}	2,21	S^-_{opt-5}	0,89

Table 5. Ranking of the alternative e-government websites

E-Government Website		Similarity Indices	RANKING
EFKA	C^*_{opt-1}	0,04	5
ERMIS-KEP	C^*_{opt-2}	0,86	2
GSIS	C^*_{opt-3}	0,88	1
DEI	C^*_{opt-4}	0,85	3
GEODATA	C^*_{opt-5}	0,29	4

6. DISCUSSION AND CONCLUSION

This paper describes an empirical evaluation of e-government websites using the combination of two Multi Criteria Decision Making theories, AHP and TOPSIS. The experiment has been implemented using five Greek e-government websites that have been evaluated before (Kabassi 2018). However, this experiment differentiates from the previous experiment in many aspects. First, the older experiment used an inspection method of evaluation using expert users instead of real potential users, which are used when an empirical method of evaluation is implemented. Empirical methods may be more successful in capturing end user's perceptions as real users participate in the experiment.

A second difference of the current experiment with the previous one (Kabassi 2018) is that the latter used only AHP to implement the evaluation experiment while this experiment uses a combination of AHP with TOPSIS. AHP is based on pairwise comparisons while TOPSIS is based on the similarity of each alternative with an ideal alternative. The selection of the Multi-Criteria Decision Making theory influences the way the experiment is implemented and the estimations are made. In this experiment, we have used the implementation of AHP with the expert users described in (Kabassi 2018) for the selection of the criteria and the estimation of their weights and have implemented TOPSIS with the participation of 30 real potential users of the e-gov websites.

A limitation of an evaluation experiment when only AHP is used is that the particular theory is a time-consuming technique because of the mathematical calculations and the number of pairwise comparisons which increase as the number of alternatives and criteria increases or changes (Jadhav & Sonar 2011). Since complexity rises with the increase of websites, it is proposed that only a few (under 10) e-government websites should be compared in each evaluation experiment that uses AHP. This is not a problem when AHP is combined with TOPSIS since there are not pairwise comparisons and each website is evaluated separately.

The implementation of the specific experiment, which involved the evaluation of e-government in Greece, revealed that GSIS was considered to be the best. The specific website is used by almost anyone in Greece as there are services related to the taxes that are implemented only through this website. This fact together with the fact that users believed that privacy and security were better on this website than all the other websites are probably the main factors why this website was rated as best. However, the similarity indices to the ideal alternative of the websites of ERMIS-KEP and DEI did not have a big difference from the first one, and, therefore considered almost equally good. ERMIS can implement a set of services that are usually implemented in KEP (Civil Services Centers) and DEI is used for paying bills and managing services related to the electricity. These websites are also used very commonly and have been improved the last years. Then, as fourth was rated the website of GEODATA. The specific open source website has a user-friendly interface where the users easily find information and geospatial data in different formats. However, most of the users participating the experiment had not used this website before contrary to the websites ranked as top three. This may be a good reason why this website was rated fourth by potential users while expert users rated as the best (Kabassi 2018).

It is our future plan to implement the experiment with more e-government website and more real users and compare their results with other similar experiments.

REFERENCES

Boussarhan, I., & Daoudi, N. (2014). The Accessibility of Moroccan Public Websites: Evaluation of Three E-Government Websites. Electronic. *Journal of e-Government, 12(1)*, 67-81.

Burmaoglu, S., & Kazancoglu, Y. (2012). E-government website evaluation with hybrid MCDM method in fuzzy environment. *International Journal of Applied Decision Sciences 5(2)*, 163-181.

Büyüközkan, G., & Ruan, D. (2007). Evaluating government websites based on a fuzzy multiple criteria decision-making approach. *International Journal of Uncertainty, Fuzziness and Knowledge-Based Systems, 15(3)*, 321–343.

Byun, D.-H., & Finnie, G. (2011) An AHP method for evaluating usability of electronic government portals. *Electronic Government, An International Journal, 8(4)*, 343-362.

Davoli, P., Mazzoni, F., & Corradini, E. (2005). Quality Assessment of Cultural Web Sites with Fuzzy Operators. *Journal of Computer Information Systems, 46(1)*, 44-57.

Dominic, P. D. D., & Jati, H. (2010) Evaluation method of Malaysian university website: Quality website using hybrid method. *International Symposium in Information Technology (ITSim)*, doi: 10.1109/ITSIM.2010.5561363.

Hwang, C. L., & Yoon, K. (1981). Multiple Attribute Decision Making: Methods and Applications. *Lecture Notes in Economics and Mathematical Systems, 186.*

Jadhav, A. S., & Sonar, R. (2011). Framework for evaluation and selection of the software packages: A hybrid knowledge based system approach. *Journal of Systems and Software, 84,* 1394–1407.

Kaaya, J. (2004). Implementing e-government services in East Africa: Assessing status through content analysis of government websites. *Electronic Journal of E-government, 2(1),* 39-54.

Kabassi, K., (2009). Fuzzy Simple Additive Weighting for Evaluating a Personalised Geographical Information System, In E. Damiani et al. (Eds.): *New Directions in Intelligent Interactive Multimedia Systems, SCI 226,* 275–284.

Kabassi, K., Alepis, E. & Virvou, M. 2011. Evaluating an Affective e-Learning System using a Fuzzy Decision Making Method. *4th International Conference on Intelligent Interactive Multimedia Systems and Services – KES-IIMSS 2011, Smart Innovation, Systems and Technologies, 11,* 177-186.

Kabassi, K. (2017). Evaluating Websites of Museums: State of the Art. *Journal of Cultural Heritage, 24,* 184-196.

Kabassi, K. (2018). AHP for Evaluating e-Government: Analysis and Application. *The Analytic Hierarchy Process: Advances in Research and Applications, nova publisher,* 175-200.

Karoulis, A., Sylaiou, S., & White, M. (2006). Usability Evaluation of a Virtual Museum Interface. *Informatica, 17(3),* 363–380.

Kaylor, C. Deshazo, R. & Van Eck, D. (2002). Gauging e-government: a report on implementing services among American cities. *Government Information Quarterly, 18(4),* 293-307.

Kunstelj, M. & Vintar, M. (2004). Evaluating the progress of e-government development: A critical analysis, *Information Policy, 9(3-4)*, 131–148.

Lewis, Cl., & Rieman, J. (1994). *Task-centered User Interface Design: A Practical Introduction*. Boulder: University of Colorado, 1994.

Liu,, J., & Wang, Y. (2008). On the Study of Project Evaluation of Websites of E-Government Procurement of China. *4th International Conference on Wireless Communications, Networking and Mobile Computing*.

Liu, M., Wang Z., & Xie H. (2010) Evaluation of E-government Web Site. *International Conference on Computer Design and Applications, 5,* 432-434.

Liu, J., & Wang Y. (2008) On the Study of Project Evaluation of Websites of EGovernment Procurement of China. *4th International Conference on Wireless Communications, Networking and Mobile Computing*.

Mohamadali, N. A., & Garibaldi, J. (2011). Comparing user acceptance factors between research software and medical software using AHP and Fuzzy AHP. In: *The 11th Workshop on Computational Intelligence*, 7 - 9 September 2011, Kilburn Building.

Mulubrhan, F., Mokhtar, A. A., & Muhammad, M. (2014). Comparative Analysis between Fuzzy and Traditional Analytical Hierarchy Process. *MATEC Web of Conferences 13*.

Oni, A., Okunoye, A. & Mbarika, V. (2016). Evaluation of E-Government Implementation: The Case of State Government Websites in Nigeria. *The Electronic Journal of e-Government 14(1)*, 48-59 available online at www.ejeg.com.

Reeves, T. C. (1993). Evaluating technology-based learning. In G. M. Piskurich (Ed.), *The ASTD Handbook of Instructional Technology*. McGraw-Hill, New York. 15.1–15.32.

Saaty, T. L. (1980). *The analytic hierarchy process*. New York, NY: McGraw-Hill.

Sirah, S., Mikhailov, L., & Keane, J. A. (2015). PriEsT: an interactive decision support tool to estimate priorities from pair-wise comparison judgments. *International Transactions in Operational Research, 22(2)*, 203–382.

Sterrenberg, G. (2017). A Conceptual Framework for Evaluating E-Government Systems Success: A Service Ecosystem Approach. *Proceedings of the 50th Hawaii International Conference on System Sciences.* 2529-2538.

Tiwari, N. (2006). Using the Analytic Hierarchy Process (AHP) to identify Performance Scenarios for Enterprise Application, *Computer Measurement Group, Measure It, 4(3),*

Tongnoy, S., Rodmanee, S., & Chen, D. N. (2012). An AHP Method for Evaluating Websites Efficiency of Ministry of Agriculture and Cooperatives in Thailand. *The Second International Congress on Interdisciplinary Research and Development*, 31 May – 1 June 2012, Thailand.

United Nations Department of Economic. (2008). *United Nations E-government Survey 2008: From e-Government to Connected Governance.* http://unpan3.un.org/egovkb/portals/ egovkb/Documents/un/2008- Survey/unpan028607.pdf.

Wang X. N. (2010) The Fuzzy Comprehensive Evaluation of User-oriented Government Websites. *International Conference on Multimedia Technology, 1 - 4,* doi: 10.1109/ICMULT.2010.5629870.

Yao, J., Lin, Y., & Zaho, P. (2010). E-government Evaluation based on Citizen Satisfaction and its Implementation. *International Conference on E-Business and E-Government,* 535-538, DOI 10.1109/ICEE. 2010.143.

Zhu, Y. & Buchman, A. (2000). Evaluating and Selecting Web Sources as External Information Resources of a Data Warehouse, *The Third International Conference on Web Information Systems Engineering (WISE'00),* 149-160.

Zhu, Q., Du J., & Han, X. (2007). The Establishment and Application of Evaluation Criteria Systems for Chinese E-Government Websites, *International Conference on Wireless Communications, Networking AHP for Evaluating E-Government: Analysis and Application and*

Mobile Computing, 2007. WiCom 2007. doi: 10.1109/WICOM. 2007.936.

Zhu, F., & Liu, Y. (2011). Assessment of the information disclosure level about government website through AHP-TOPSIS method. *International Conference of Information Technology, Computer Engineering and Management Sciences*, 179-181. DOI 10.1109/ICM.2011.346.

In: e-Government
Editor: Anil Sieben

ISBN: 978-1-53617-563-9
© 2020 Nova Science Publishers, Inc.

Chapter 4

WHY AND HOW SOUTH KOREA BECAME THE WORLD'S BEST E-GOVERNMENT COUNTRY: FOCUSING ON THE LEADERSHIP OF PRESIDENT ROH, MOO-HYUN

Choong-Sik Chung
Department of Public Administration, KyungSung University
Busan, Republic of Korea

ABSTRACT

Today, South Korea is regarded as the world's best country in the field of e-government. In the most recent UN e-Government Survey conducted in 2018, South Korea ranked third after Denmark and Australia. In addition, it was ranked number one in the UN e-Government Survey three times in a row from 2010 to 2014. As such, South Korea is recognized as a global leader in e-government.

The e-government systems utilized in Korea today have been implemented and completed in the days of the Roh Moo-hyun administration. On August 14, 2003, the 'Roh Moo-hyun Administration e-Government Vision and Principles' was announced and was followed by the 'e-Government Roadmap.' The e-Government Roadmap was composed of four areas of innovation, 10 agendas, and 31 projects. During the period from 2003 to 2007, a total budget of USD 981 million was invested in e-government implementation.

President Roh, Moo-hyun's insights and intentions toward the electronic government were reflected in the e-government projects in Korea and hence Korea's electronic government policies achieved great results during the Roh Moo-hyun government. When President Roh, Moo-hyun took office in 2003, UN e-government ranking of South Korea had remained outside the top 10; it improved to be ranked 5th by the end of his term in 2008 and soon achieved world's top place by 2010.

President Roh, Moo-hyun was directly engaged as a developed in the e-Government development team to design document management and task management processes with experts. The fact that the president of a country directly participated in the development and diffusion of the e-Government system remains a rare case in the world.

As such, e-Government can be successfully pursued if the president's will and leadership are firmly established. But there is a dilemma here. Eventually, the president is replaced and the new government takes office and thus it is important to ensure the permanence of the e-government policy. In this case, it is necessary to designate a national CIO and institutionalize it, not solely depending on the ability of the president's own leadership. Therefore, the Republic of Korea is still indebted to President Roh, Moo-hyun for the success of the e-government.

INTRODUCTION

South Korea is now recognized as a global leader in e-government. But over 50 years ago, South Korea was one of the underdeveloped countries in the field of information and communication. After the Korean War in 1950, South Korea was one of the poorest countries in the world in the 1960s. However, based on its economic growth, South Korea has now established itself as a leader of e-government.

As of the end of 2018, South Korea's per capita income exceeded US $ 30,000 and has grown into the world's top 10 economy countries. At the same time, South Korea has achieved remarkable growth in the field of information and communication. After going through continuous efforts in e-Government and national informatization, Korea has become one of the global E-government leaders - obtaining the highest scores in

'E-government Development Index' and 'E-participation Index.' Korea's E-government Development Index ranking assessed by the United Nations improved from 15th in 2001 to the top in 2010 out of 192 countries worldwide, and its E-participation Index ranking was also ranked 1st in 2010, 2012, and 2014 (UN, 2010; 2012; 2014). In the most recent UN e-Government Survey conducted in 2018, South Korea ranked third after Denmark and Australia (UN, 2018). In addition, many of Korea's E-government practices until now have been introduced to the world as the best cases and have received worldwide acknowledgment. Therefore, South Korea is regarded as the world's best country in the field of e-government.

The history of e-government in South Korea is an abbreviation of Korean modern history. For the past 50 years, South Korea has emerged from the world's poorest countries and became a G20 country economically, and has established a democratic political system politically. It is a miracle that can't be found anywhere else in the history of the world. Thus this is called the miracle of the Han River.

Many people say that South Korea has become the world's best country in e-government because of its technological advancements in the field of information and communication network. But this comes from ignorance of e-government. E-government is not just the introduction of information and communication technologies, nor is it the construction of information systems. Therefore, although the establishment of high-speed information and communication infrastructure contributed greatly to the development of e-government in Korea, this alone cannot explain the success of e-government in Korea (Chung, 2019).

In order for a country's e-government to be successful, various factors must be supported. The success factors of Korean e-Government are summarized as strong political leadership, clear vision and policy objective, project's strategic priority, and human & financial resource distribution.

So far, various analyzes have been made on these success factors for Korean e-government (Song, 2002; Ahn, 2017). But the most important of these success factors is the leadership of the president. Especially in countries where there is still an administrative culture under the imperial presidential system, such as Korea, the leadership of the president has the greatest influence on policy decision making and implementation. Therefore, South Korea's e-government success was possible because of the outstanding leader, Roh Moo-hyun.

Therefore, the main object of this paper is to verify why and how Korea transformed into one of the global E-Government Leaders. Specifically, this paper examines e-government policies in the Roh Moo-hyun administration from 2003 to 2007 and analyzes them from the perspective of the leadership of the president.

SUCCESS FACTORS OF E-GOVERNMENT AND PRESIDENT LEADERSHIP

This section examines the success factors of e-government and summarizes the leadership of the president.

A Study on the Success Factors of Early E-Government by Authors in Korea

I have conducted studies on the factors that influence the success of e-government for a long time. Specifically, in Korea in 1996, I conducted three major Policy Delphi methods research against 30 experts as the target group to study the major success factors of Korean e-government implementation (Chung, 1997). At the time, as a result of these studies, the 10 major success factors of the e-government implementation were mentioned as follows.

- 1st place: Improvement of law and institutions
- 2nd place: President's leadership
- 3rd place: Changes in government processes (BPR)

- 4th place: Build DB for common use of administrative information
- 5th place: Construction of High Speed Information Communication Network
- 6th place: Digitization of administrative information
- 7th place: Development of electronic service delivery
- 8th place: Coordination of ministries' interests
- 9th place: Education of government officials
- 10th place: Establishment of the Governance

Twenty years ago, the concept of e-government was vague in Korea, and technology determinism was dominated in the promotion of electronic government policies. Nevertheless, it can be seen that socioeconomic factors accounted for the first, second, and third place of success factors. In this study, the president's leadership came second, following the "Improvement of law and institutions."

The reason why the improvement of law and institutions was mentioned as the most important success factor was because the Korean government enacted the Framework Act on Informatization Promotion in 1996 and the informatization policy was very active in the social atmosphere at the time. The importance of these laws continued and in 2001 South Korea became the first country to enact the e-government act in the world. Since then, South Korea's e-government act has had the biggest impact on Korea's e-government promotion policy, allowing South Korea to leap forward as a leader in digital government (Chung & Kim, 2019).

The leadership of the president ranked second. In the three Policy Delphi surveys, experts responded that the leadership of the president was an important success factor since e-government was not just a single department's informatization project, but it also involved innovating the processes of different ministries. In Korea's case, since most of the administrative power was concentrated on one president, many experts suggested that the leadership of the president was crucial in resolving conflicts and selfishness among ministries in the promotion of e-government. In subsequent studies of e-government success factors conducted in Korea, the president's leadership has always been mentioned as a high priority (Song & Cho, 2007).

Success Factors of the US Clinton Administration's E-Government

The term e-government first appeared in the world in September 1993. The term e-government was first used in *"Reengineering Through Information Technology,"* a report published by NPR in the United States. In this way, the concept of e-government in the United States was introduced to enhance the rationality of the decision-making process using ICT and to implement the citizen-oriented government.

In 1993, NPR presented the following 13 initiatives as a concrete way for the federal government to implement e-government (NPR, 1993).

- Strengthen Leadership in Information Technology
  - IT01: Provide Clear, Strong Leadership to Integrate Information Technology into the Business of Government
- Implement Electronic Government
  - IT02: Implement Nationwide, Integrated Electronic Benefit Transfer
  - IT03: Develop Integrated Electronic Access to Government Information and Services
  - IT04: Establish a National Law Enforcement/Public Safety Network
  - IT05: Provide Intergovernmental Tax Filing, Reporting, and Payments Processing
  - IT06: Establish an International Trade Data System
  - IT07: Create a National Environmental Data Index
  - IT08: Plan, Demonstrate, and Provide Government wide Electronic Mail
- Establish Support Mechanisms for Electronic Government
  - IT09: Improve Government's Information Infrastructure

- IT10: Develop Systems and Mechanisms to Ensure Privacy and Security
- IT11: Improve Methods of Information Technology Acquisition
- IT12: Provide Incentives for Innovation
- IT13: Provide Training and Technical Assistance in Information Technology to Federal Employees

These 13 action plans consisted of 47 specific action items and were continuously implemented from 1993 to 1997. Leadership was the first of these 13 e-government action plans of the first Clinton administration. The content is as follows.

IT01: Provide Clear, Strong Leadership to Integrate Information Technology into the Business of Government

The content of IT01 is about how to secure leadership in US government reform. More important in government reform is not the information technology but the leadership that can be implemented. This means today's ICT governance. To this end, the Clinton administration embodied the NPR vision and upgraded the use of IT to a national goal.

Lesson from the United Stated Case

The greatest lesson learned from e-government success during the Clinton administration in the United States is leadership. The most important part of the process of implementing e-government in many countries or establishing a national digital governance strategy was the introduction and utilization of ICT. However, the lesson that can be gained from the success stories of the United States is that e-government implementation required strong leadership in order to achieve administrative innovation in the public sector using ICT.

In fact, in 1993, the United States President Clinton convened high-level officials of the federal government in the White House where he was responsible for economic, diplomatic, security, and security issues while the field of environmental and informatization was delegated to Vice

President Al Gore. In addition, since the appointment of Vice President Al Gore as the head of the NPR, the Government of the United States which used information technology was led by El Gore for eight years (Kamensky, 1996). As a result, the E-Government initiatives and government reforms were carried out with a strong force and persistence, as the president delegated authority to the vice president who exercised full authority.

Success Factors of e-Government and Leadership

Since the success of e-government in the United States in 1993, many countries have been pushing for e-government policies. In the process, a variety of global ICT companies, consulting firms, and international organizations have published reports on e-government initiatives. The major success factors of e-government suggested in these reports are as follows.

IBM (1999)

In July 1999, IBM Corporation presented the vision and strategy of e-government (Caldow, 1999). The report criticized the e-government as being too narrowly defined and argued that it should be broadly defined, including digital democracy. According to this report, in order for e-government to be implemented, the following components must be combined, individually or in combination, with the overall technology strategy.

- Leadership
- Policy
- Economic Competitiveness
- Citizen Services
- Intranet & Extranet
- Community
- Digital Democracy
- Pulling it All Together -- Technology Behind the Scenes

As such, leadership has been suggested as one of the most important success factors in e-government. In particular, this report has great significance by extending the implementation of e-government to the level of digital democracy.

Deloitte (2000)

In 2000, Deloitte Consulting published a report entitled "At the Dawn of e-GOVERNMENT: The Citizen as Customer" (Deloitte Research, 2000). This report was the result of an empirical study of a top-management perspective from more than 250 state-level government departments in Australia, Canada, New Zealand, the United Kingdom, and the United States.

Deloitte presented a checklist that should be considered when planning e-government. The checklist can be summarized as follows:

- Define a Vision – and a Business Case – for e-Government
- Build Customer Trust with Privacy, Security and Confidentiality
- Plan Technology for Growth and Customer-Friendliness
- Manage Access Channels to Optimise Value
- Weigh In-Sourcing vs. Outsourcing
- Establish Investment Plans That Work Within Funding Cycles
- Understand the Impact of Fees for Transactions
- Include a Strong Change Management Program
    - Leadership with Commitment:
    - Shared Vision of e-Government:
    - Customer Outreach:

Deloitte's emphasis on the strong change management program includes leadership with commitment. Emphasizing that the transition to e-government is not an easy task, it explains the government leadership necessary for e-government success as follows.

Leadership must be a diverse group of high-ranking officials – including governors/ministers, CIOs, department heads and members of legislatures – that collectively endorses and provides the resources to facilitate the transition to the e-Government model. The group must also have a single champion driving the initiative.

Accenture (2001)

Since 2000, Accenture has been measuring eGovernment Leadership (Accenture, 2001). In 2001, Accenture conducted research in 22 countries around the world with the following questions. What progress has been made in the development of eGovernment? What actions have national governments taken to turn their vision into reality? What opportunities exist for countries to truly exhibit eGovernment Leadership?

Accenture evaluated e-government maturity in 22 countries around the world. The e-government maturity was measured by dividing the e-government service aspect (service maturity) and the delivery system aspect (delivery maturity) to deliver the service.

Accenture found that political leaders were increasingly commenting on the merits of online government, yet this was not translating into action. Accenture suggested the importance of leadership in the promotion of e-government:

> Interestingly, the research found that overall progress in eGovernment is not closely correlated with similar social, political or economic characteristics. Leadership, political will, commitment to deliverables and accountability for results are the factors that appear to have the greatest influence on progress. The early adopters of eGovernment, driven by these factors, have achieved greater sophistication in online service delivery, while countries that are only now articulating their vision have the opportunity to make up ground and learn from the lessons of the leaders.
>
> Tomorrow's eGovernment leaders will match strong political will with co-ordinated action. Whole of Government guiding principles are required to ensure that through cross agency co-operation, a framework for customer focused, service provision emerges.

OECD (2003)

In a report published in 2003, the OECD emphasized leadership as an imperative for e-government initiatives (OECD, 2003). However, OECD pointed out that the implementation of e-government is difficult, risky, and expensive so that government innovation through e-government has many obstacles and is expensive.

It also argued that the nature of e-government promotion requires the leadership of various characteristics at various levels in order to cope with rapidly changing technologies and to remove various obstacles. The OECD proposed the principles of successful e-government leadership as follows (OECD, 2003: 98).

- Co-ordinating resources and responsibilities within the organization
- Developing a common vision and set objectives (e-agenda)
- Developing the ability to persuade people to that vision in order to convince the enthusiasts and engage the sceptics
- Developing a customer-led and customer-focused approach
- Ensuring that leadership can be recognized and encouraged wherever it is found in the organization
- Raising the awareness and developing the skills of employees, encouraging innovative solutions to organizational problems
- Assessing and building the capacity to deliver online service, leading people through the difficult process of change, securing the commitment from staff along the way and managing their programme of work
- Ensuring technological development within the organization and make sure that personnel can fully benefits from that
- Recognising that full use of technologies but not chasing technological solution in itself

What is particularly noteworthy about this report is that it provides examples of Korea's success in the area of leadership. This report describes the success of the 2002 e-government promotion committee rather than a single ministry in the e-government process in South Korea (OECD, 2003: 95).

E-Government Initiatives in the Roh Administration (2003-2007)

The e-government systems utilized in Korea today have been implemented and completed in the days of the Roh Moo-hyun administration. Focusing on the Roh government, the contents of the e-government initiatives carried out at the time are as follows.

Historical Overview of Korean E-Government Promotion

In relation to the history of e-government promotion in Korea, researchers can make varying distinctions regarding the development phases. In particular, the 50th anniversary of e-government in Korea was held in 2017, led by the government (MOIS, 2017b). In this case, the origin of the Korean e-government was traced back to 1967. However, as shown in Table 1, the distinction here is made in terms of government innovation using information technology rather than computerization and informatization.

Prior to E-government Promotion

The promotion of e-government in Korea has historically been divided into before and after e-government that started in 2000. Prior to 2000, Korea had been promoting national computerization, national networking, and national informatization projects but not the e-government. The full-fledged beginning of e-government in Korea can be seen in 2001 as shown in Table 1. The computerization and informatization before 2000 are summarized as follows.

Table 1. History of Korea e-government implementation

Stage	Main Implementation contents
ICT Initial Stage (1960s ~ 1970s)	• Introduction of computers to the statistics business of Economic Planning Board (1967) • Administration ICT 5 year basic plan establishment (1978)
e-Government incubation period (1980s ~ 1990s)	• Administration ICT business (NBIS) • National period of computing network business (1987)
e-Government base preparation period (mid 1990s ~ 2000)	• Establishment of Ultra High Speed information communication base • Framework enactment on ICT Implementation law
e-Government starting period (2001 ~ 2002)	• Implement e-Government 11 tasks • Enact laws on e-Government (2001)
e-Government growth period (2003 ~ 2007)	• Implementation of e-Government-31 tasks • Prepared the base for linking and integrating government institutions and departments
e-Government maturity period (2008 ~ 2012)	• National ICT master plan establishment (2008) • Implement e-Government 12 tasks based on opening, sharing and cooperation of businesses.
Intelligent e-Government period (2013 ~ Present)	• National ICT master plan establishment (2008) • Implement e-Government 12 tasks based on opening, sharing and cooperation of businesses. • Act on Promotion of the Provision and Use of Public Data (2013) • Intelligent Government Plan (2017) • AI National Strategy (2019)

Source: Chung, 2015 Modified.

Korea's informatization began in the late 1970s when major administrative business processes were computerized in the areas including resident registration, real-estate, and vehicles. In the 1990s, the focus of informatization shifted to unit-based or function-based processes such as those for passport patent and procurement administration.

Between 1992 and 1994 when the government structure was in transit from a totalitarian government to a congressional government, the interest in IT development by President Kim Young-Sam somewhat diminished; however, with the launch of Information Superhighway Project in USA in 1993, the government solidified its will once more by newly establishing the Ministry of Information & Communication (MIC) and through the High Speed Broadband Network Project.

Kim, Dae-jung Administration (Jan. 2001-Jan. 2003)

During 1998-2000, right after the Asian financial crisis, President Kim Dae-Jung's interests were focused on the restructuring of 4 major sectors to recover from the economic crisis and therefore the president's interest in e-government project was lowered. But from 2001, the president's will and interest solidified the e-Government Project as the strategic enabler with highest importance for government innovation.

Establishment of the E-government Promotion Committee - Upgrading E-Government to Presidential Agenda (January 2001)

The Korean government established the Special Committee of e-Government on January 30, 2001 in order to promote interagency collaboration in negotiating issues concerning the e-Government initiatives.

Table 2. E-Government vision and strategy of Kim, Dae-Jung Administration

Vision	e-Government to make the transition to a world-class nation • A government that provides the best quality administrative service for the people • A government that provides the most suitable environment for business activities • A government with maximum productivity, transparency, and democracy
Strategy	• To redesign administrative process to cope with the flow of information and establish information system • To establish one-stop window for e-Government and support for unified process of civil services • To establish administrative networks, improve institutions and form an information infrastructure

Source: SCEG, 2003.

The Special Committee for e-Government was established as a special committee under the Presidential Commission on Government Innovation, which is an executive branch committee. Therefore, the Special Committee for e-Government reported to the president as an independent body.

The Special Committee for e-Government proposed a vision and strategy in May 2001, as shown in Table 2.

Enactment of the E-Government Act (July 2001)

After President Kim Dae-jung's Millennium New Year message of 2000, e-government became a national agenda. Subsequently, in March 2000, the Ministry of Government Administration and Home Affairs reported that the government would enact e-government laws while reporting to the President. Until this time no nation in the world had ever enacted a single law related to e-government, but the Kim Dae-jung government prepared to enact the e-government law. The law was drafted in June 2000 and passed the legislative process in the autumn of 2000. The law was promulgated in March 2001 and came into force in July 2001.

The main details include the following: First, the basic principles for the implementation of e-Government policy; second, provision and utilization of e-Government services (including electronic processing of civil services such as provision/utilization of e-Government services); third, construction and utilization of hubs for e-documents, administrative digital signatures, and construction and utilization of common infrastructure system; fourth, adoption and utilization of information technology architecture and laying the groundwork for efficient management of information resources; fifth, pre-consultation for the implementation of the e-Government projects, performance analysis and diagnosis, international cooperation, designation of a dedicated agency, etc. (MOIS, 2017b: 50).

Establishment of the E-government Infrastructure - 11 Projects Completed (November 2002)

The Kim Dae-jung government formed a Special Committee for e-Government under the direct control of the President and, since 2001, promoted 11 e-government initiatives for two years. The contents are summarized as shown in Table 3.

President Kim, Dae-Jung held a meeting for the 'Report on the Completion of e-Government Infrastructure' on November 13, 2002 with all ministers from each participating ministries in attendance. President Kim announced that 11 major e-Government initiatives were successfully executed and declared the opening of full-scale e-Government services (SCEG, 2003). Therefore, the Special Committee for e-Government was dissolved as of January 31, 2003.

The successful completion of the 11 e-Government initiatives brought many changes to how the government operated and had a positive impact on citizens and private businesses. The inefficient use of the budget and human resources that were allocated to outdated procedures and functions were reduced substantially. Efficient government services boosted productivity of private businesses and lessened the burden on civil servants who no longer had to process redundant procedures. The level of national competitiveness improved in the long-term due to these e-Government initiatives.

Table 3. 11 E-Government Initiatives in Korea

Objective	Main Features
Upgrade Government-wide service for Citizen and private business	① Government for Citizen (G4C) System ② Social Insurance Information Sharing System ③ Home Tax Service System ④ Government e-Procurement System
Improve the effectiveness of Administration	⑤ National Finance Information System ⑥ National Education Information System ⑦ Local Government Information Network System ⑧ Personnel Policy Support System
Establish an Infrastructure for e-Government	⑨ e-Approval & e-Document Exchange ⑩ e-Signature & e-Seal System ⑪ Government-wide Integrated Computer Network

Source: SCEG, 2003: 13.

Roh Moo-Hyun Administration (2003-2007)

Moo-hyun Roh, who took office in February 2003, was the 16th President of the Republic of Korea. President Roh, Moo-hyun had extraordinary insights into and understanding of the fields of information policy and e-government. Therefore, the Roh Moo-hyun administration started to look very different from the previous administrations. From the early days of his administration, he strongly pursued information policy and e-government projects with the leadership of the president. Today, Korea has the highest position in the world in the field of digital government because of the accomplishments of the Roh Moo-hyun administration.

Strongly Implemented from the Beginning of the Regime: Clear Vision and Goals

Prior to the Roh administration, both Kim Young-sam and Kim Dae-jung administrations implemented information policy and digital government-related projects in the latter half of the administration. Given the loss of power in the latter half of the ruling party's term, policies that were pursued were difficult to receive firm support. Therefore, it can't be said that they recognized the importance of information policy and digital government promotion in a timely manner.

However, the Roh administration showed a totally different start. As soon as the Roh Moo-hyun administration took office it selected five major national agendas, one of which was the e-government. As a result, the e-government was recognized as a presidential project from the beginning and had a strong driving force. On the basis of this, the Roh Moo-hyun government established the vision and strategy of e-government linked to the national ideology at the beginning of the term. The Roh Moo-hyun administration's vision and goals for e-government are as shown in Table 4 (PCGID, 2003).

Table 4. E-Government vision and strategy of Roh, Moo-Hyun Administration

Vision	Realize World's highest level of open e-Government
	• Innovate service to the people => Network Government
	• Enhance administrative efficiency, transparency => Knowledge Government
	• Realize true sovereignty of the people => Participatory Government
Objective	• Build a value creation type or information system for the people and corporations
	• Maximize result within the government and improve efficiency
	• Form a horizontal two-way network between the people and the government

The firm resolve of the Participatory Government gave birth to the E-Government Roadmap, which aimed to realize Korea's vision of becoming the "World's Best Open E-Government" and was largely made up of the following two goals.

First, The phrase "World's Best" was the realization of Korea as the world's top-class nation based on Korea's recent achievements in ICT areas.

Second, "Open E-Government" was the vision of a true participatory democracy realized by participation of the people in policy formulation and government administration processes through transparent public administration. These two components in realizing "World's Best Open E-Government" greatly helped the Korean effort to rise to the level of advanced nations in both political and administrative landscapes. It also led to three very concrete concepts for E-Government.

- Establishment of a network-based government through the innovation of public service delivery
- Realization of a knowledge-based government through transparent and efficient public administration
- Realization of a participatory government through true democracy

The three major goals for achieving this vision were:

- Reform of Government Administration: Replace paper document processing with electronic document processing method, while stand-alone government information systems will be integrated into a one-stop information system
- Reform of Citizen Service Delivery: Citizens no longer need to visit government offices for receiving civil services but instead conveniently access government services through a single online window
- Reform of Information Resource Management: Information resources such as human resources, organization, budget, and information systems, which were managed separately by the respective agencies in the past, will be integrated across the government by using a common standard to ensure interoperability among systems.

31 E-Government Projects Roadmap (2003 – 2007)

On August 14, 2003, the 'Roh Administration e-Government Vision and Principles' was announced, followed by the 'e-Government Roadmap'. The e-Government Roadmap is composed of four areas of innovation, 10 agendas, and 31 projects as shown in Table 5 (MOGAHA, 2006: 12-34).

1. Digitalizing Document Processing Procedures: A supporting system for e-document exchange is expected to ensure efficiency, security, and reliability in administration, along with a paperless environment, and is to be utilized as a base system in realizing e-government.
2. Comprehensive Informatization of National and Local Public Finance: National finance will be integrated and managed under the Digital Budget & Accounting System, which was adopted as a national agenda, separate from the e-government roadmap projects. Local finance informatization will be processed with the establishment of a standard information system according to

international standards, leading to real-time business processing. In line with this project, BPR/ISP for local finance informatization was carried out in 2004, which resulted in four core tasks being identified for local finance informatization and innovation.

3. Realizing Local E-Government: Local e-government projects for city/province are expected to connect the central and upper/lower local governments, improve the administrative systems of city/province administrations, and increase efficiency. They also aim at reducing paper-based civil documents and establishing infrastructure where services can be offered regardless of time, place, or device.

Table 5. 31 E-Government Roadmap Projects

Area	Agenda	Projects
Innovating The Way Government Work	1. Establishing Electronic Work Process	1. Electronic Document Processing
		2. Consolidated Financial Information System
		3. Local e-Government
		4. e-Auditing System
		5. e-National Assembly
		6. Integrated Criminal Justice Services
		7. Consolidated Personnel Administration System
		8. e-Diplomacy System
		9. Real-time System for National Policy Management
	2. Expanding the Administrative Information	10. Expansion of the Administrative Information Sharing System
	3. Service-oriented Business Process Reengineering	11. Government Business Reference Model(BRM) Development

Area	Agenda	Projects
Innovating Civil Services	4. Enhancing Citizen Service	12. Enhanced Online Citizen Services
		13. Integrated National Disaster Management Services
		14. Consolidated Architectural Administrative Information System
		15. Consolidated Online Tax System
		16. Integrated National Welfare Services
		17. Consolidated Food and Drug Information System
		18. Consolidated Employment Information Services
		19. Online Administrative Trial System
	5. Enhancing Business Support Services	20. One-stop Business Support Services(G4B)
		21. Consolidated National Logistics Information Services
		22. Electronic Trading Services
		23. Comprehensive Foreigner Support Services
		24. Support for Exporting of E-Government Solutions
	6. Enhancing Online Citizen Participation	25. Expansion of Online Citizen Participation
Innovating Information Resource Management	7. Consolidating and Standardizing Information Resources	26. Government-wide Consolidated Information Resources Administration System
		27. Enhancement of e-Government Communication Network
		28. Establishment of Government-wide Information Technology Architecture
	8. Strengthening Information Security Systems	29. Establishment of Information Security System
	9. Strengthening Capacity of IT Personnel and Organizations	30. Restructuring of IT Personnel and Organizations
Reforming the Legal System	10. Reforming e-Government Related Legal Systems	31. Reform of e-Government Legal System

4. Building e- Auditing System: In 2003, the Board of Audit and Inspection(BAI) drew up a plan for innovative auditing operations aiming at customer satisfaction and productive and transparent auditing processes in order to respond to the changing environment where auditing data was also digitized, performance-oriented management systems were established in government agencies, and double-entry bookkeeping was introduced. The e-auditing system is an outcome of the plan, with a view of preventing redundancy in auditing and ensuring expertise and efficiency with efficient knowledge management. In addition, it also aims at assisting proactive auditing and performance-oriented auditing with the establishment of a system of data collecting, analysis, and assessment by connecting administrative information systems.
5. Realizing e-National Assembly: The legislature has three visions for e-Assembly (networked Assembly, participatory Assembly, and knowledge-based Assembly). The concept of a networked Assembly is to connect the National Assembly and all other related institutions in order to effectively share information. An Online Document Proposal System on parliamentary politics is an absolute means for that. Every institution included in the network can request or submit official documents such as bills, budgets, closing accounts as well as other information via the Internet.
6. Building an Integrated Criminal Justice Service System: There existed a system in operation for supporting criminal proceedings that was widely used in the entire criminal process from investigation to prosecution. This system was used by many agencies including the police, Ministry of Labor, Customs Service, National Tax Service, National Intelligence Service, courts, and the Ministry of Justice. However, there have been complaints that individual visits to separate agencies are still often required in the case of many criminal proceedings. In an effort to address this problem it was proposed that information from all agencies should be consolidated and all processes related to criminal proceedings should be put into a single network by using the latest ICT

technologies. The criminal investigation service should be able to support all tasks related to criminal proceedings. In order to fully digitize work processes, a standardized system promoting the use of common information would need to be set up, along with the construction of a portal site to convert the in-place criminal investigation service into a fully unified system.

7. Comprehensive Informatization of HR Management: The human resources (HR) information system for local governments enables such HR affairs as payrolls, organization management, and training to be processed in an integrated manner among local governments, with the aim of increasing the efficiency of HR administrations.

8. e-Diplomacy System: With the necessity to efficiently adapt to rapid changes in the international environment and provide timely support for core work processes, the Ministry of Foreign Affairs and Trade (MOFAT) established the e-Diplomacy project. In line with this project, civil services were improved with the establishment of the e-diplomacy and e-consul systems. The e-document exchange system was also established among the ministries and embassies abroad.

9. Real-time Management of National Agenda: The e-Knowledge Management System enables various ideas and knowledge proposed in the process of policy-making to be recorded and managed, aiming at sharing diverse policy information through e-document management and government work and coordinating support for efficient decision-making. The Government Work Management Systems refer to the Government Business Reference Model and the Business Process Management System.

10. Expanding of Administrative Information Sharing: The administrative information sharing system makes it possible for public agencies and financial institutions as well as government agencies to process civil applications with the direct identification of certificates. Administrative information sharing would be available for 70 services frequently used by citizens, thereby

leading to a reduction of about 67 percent in paper-based documents.

11. Developing Government Business Reference Model: The Government Business Reference Model (BRM) is a framework that is systematically structured according to the government service and business processes, upon classifying government functions by their goals and performance rather than the ministries in charge of such functions. It identifies all government functions and maps each of them with its related organization, laws, budget, and information systems. It re-classifies the functions according to goals, parties concerned, and service types for round-the-clock management.

12. Enhancing Internet-based Civil Services: The Government for Citizen (G4C) project, which was launched in 2000, is aimed to enable citizens to have easy access to the necessary information, and to use one-stop online civil services regardless of time and place. These G4C services have become accessible since 2002, offering guidelines for approximately 4,400 kinds of civil services and 393 kinds of civil applications through the web. Since 2004, the online issuances of civil certificates, including certificates of residence, have been available. In line with this enhancing effort, the number of online civil services and their quality will continue to be increased.

13. Integrated National Disaster Management Service: To prevent natural and artificial disasters and minimize the damages incurred by them, an efficient national emergency management system needs to be developed. Based on this understanding, the government organized the National Emergency Management Agency (NEMA) as the agency responsible for disaster management, with a focus on prevention-oriented disaster management rather than reconstruction and compensation. The purpose of the National Disaster Management System (NDMS) is to systemically support the management of disaster prevention, preparation, responsiveness, and rehabilitation.

14. **Advanced Architectural Administration Information System**: The Architecture Administration Information System (AIS) enables the electronic processing of all aspects of administrative processes related to architecture, housing, and management of construction, and it uses information gathered in the AIS processing to generate diverse documents such as building registers, search electronic blueprints, and provide information on related policies and statistics on a real-time basis. With the development of AIS in 1998, those seeking architectural approvals do not need to submit thousands of hand-drawn blueprints any more, nor visit related offices.
15. **Integrated Tax Service**: The goal of the consolidated online tax system is to facilitate the use of the Home Tax Service in a more convenient way, which enables taxpayers to take all proceedings related to tax notices, tax reference, tax payments, and records online without the need to visit tax offices. The Home Tax Service has been offering the services since 2002, designed in 2001 as one of the 11 key initiatives. Out of 14 national tax items, 12 most frequently used services can be applied and paid online by the use of the Home Tax Service.
16. **Integrated National Welfare Service**: Integrated national welfare services provide information on national welfare services efficiently, especially to socially vulnerable groups such as the disabled, children, women, and the elderly. A model was established to efficiently support social welfare services by devising an informatization strategy for the development of a national welfare information system in 2004.
17. **Comprehensive Food and Drug Information Service**: The need for an information management and service system has fast become apparent, in order to integrate food and drug safety management work processes with data that was dispersed among the Korea Food and Drug Administration, central government agencies, and local governments. In line with this plan, in 2005 an information

system for food safety management was established, enabling citizens to handle service procedures through the Internet.
18. Comprehensive Employment Information Service: Comprehensive Employment Information Services are being carried out under three different projects: integrated information on labor markets, user-oriented information, and a Labor Market Analysis System (LaMAS). This project aims to provide a base for the effective innovation of public service delivery to citizens and implementation of the government's unemployment measures by building an information system that provides comprehensive employment information. In so doing, information on the labor market, such as employment insurance, job training, qualifications for various agencies, and computer networks are reorganized and provided in an integrated manner to meet user demands.
19. Internet-based Administrative Judgement Service: The administrative trial services are ensuring a remedy for the violations when the rights of the people are infringed by government agencies, including unfair administrative procedures and official misconduct. In the year 2004, the "Internet-based Administrative Judgment System Development Project" was carried out. In addition to the administrative ruling Internet application notification system, which electronically registers and notifies applicants on a real-time basis through the Internet, the administrative ruling work process informatization system and administrative ruling knowledge information service system have been developed.
20. Single-Window for Business Support Services (G4B): The G4B services provide one-stop e-government service to businesses including corporate civil administrative affairs, industrial information, and other additional services on various activities throughout the corporate life cycle of an enterprise from its establishment to its closure. This project was divided into three areas: formulation of the G4B Vision and mid- to long-term

development strategy; establishment of a system development strategy for G4B projects; and building the G4B pilot system.

21. Integrated National Logistics Information Service: The national logistics information services are expected to improve the business processes of logistics and provide user-oriented logistic services by standardizing similar or duplicated logistic documents and increasing information-sharing among related agencies. The establishment of a user-oriented portal, information-sharing, and establishment of consolidated logistics information services for informatization will continue to be implemented. Consequently, this project resulted in cost reduction in personnel, budget, and time management by standardizing logistics documents and increasing information-sharing.

22. E-Commerce Service: The e-Trade services are to support seamless processing of all aspects of trade affairs such as marketing, foreign exchange, customs, and logistics. In order to strengthen national competitiveness for export, a new paradigm for trade was required, along with the early establishment of an e-trade platform. The National e-Trade Committee was organized under the chair of the Prime Minister in 2003, in order to enhance e-trade projects in an efficient manner, and released a master plan for national e-trade. Beginning with the establishment of an e-trade document repository, the 'e-Letter of Credit (e-L/C) Distribution Management System' is currently in operation. This project enabled the notice, transfer, and buying application of e-L/C as a world first, which resulted in eliminating the need for paper-based L/C, and preventing the loss, damage, or forgery of the L/C.

23. Comprehensive Foreigner Support Service: The Ministry of Commerce, Industry, and Energy (MOCIE), the Ministry of Labor (MOLAB), and the Ministry of Justice(MOJ) have taken lead of this project, in order to provide the benefits of e-government to foreigners by initiating 'Government for Foreigners(G4F)' services, to increase their convenience in immigration, entry/departure and overseas investment. The three business areas,

which include foreign investment, entry/departure/stay, and employment, were redesigned. The service system will be provided both in English and Korean.

24. Support for Exporting E-Government Solutions: This project has been carried out with a special focus on publicizing Korea's e-government experiences and good practices to other countries and facilitating domestic industries' investments related to e-government. Overseas promotion of e-government solutions for businesses and international cooperation is being carried out according to the role played by each agency. Under this project, consulting and feasibility studies have been conducted on e-government in developing countries, along with human resource exchanges and international promotional events.

25. Increasing Online Citizen Participation: In order to establish a foundation for a citizen participation-oriented public administration, under which an interactive channel will reflect the voice of the public from all parts of society and allow citizen participation in policy administration, information creation and decision making (PAID by the people: Policy, Administration, Information, Decision By the People), the government carried out system development. The Citizen Participation portal (www.epeople.go.kr) started a trial service integrating relevant areas of the Internet Newsgroup (civil complaint petition) of the Blue House, Participation Newsgroup (citizen proposals and policy participation), and the Ombudsman of Korea (civil complaints and proposals) in 2005.

26. Building a Government-wide NCIA: The National Computing & Information Administration (NCIA) project is implemented to integrate information resources including information systems and personnel matters separately run by each government agency, and ultimately enhance information sharing and efficiency. Furthermore, it establishes interchangeable dual backup systems to efficiently respond to any type of accident. The systems from a total of 48 agencies will be moved to the first and second NCIA

centers. 24 agencies completed their transfer of systems to the first center by 2006 and the systems are currently operating without any issues. The second center was constructed in 2007 and additional 24 agencies transferred their systems to the second center.

27. Strengthening E-Government Communications Network (e-GOV Net): The enhancement of the e-Government Communications Network is to construct secure, stable and viable communication networks only for the use of government agencies, thereby providing quality-guaranteed ICT services at a reasonable cost to citizens. It also aims at establishing efficient communication channels among government agencies, citizens and businesses, and providing convenient and efficient e-government services. Project plans were established to organize the e-government networks that share the facilities of communication providers, and also to construct an IP-based interconnection network operated with governments' direct investments, which are currently in operation.

28. Establishing Government-wide ITA: This project aims to make all the government agencies use the ITA, which supports the systematic and standardized management of informatization by government agencies, in order to increase the efficiency of informatization. The ITA performance is systematically organized and the information is provided to the agencies that introduced the ITA. Plans are also made for the further introduction of the ITA by other agencies.

29. Building an Information Security System: With the increased circulation and volume of e-government related classified documents, the need to establish a Government Key Management Infrastructure (GKMI) became increasingly apparent. Electronic Certification System Enhancement Project aimed to improve identity verification and secure circulation systems in order to increase the trustworthiness and safety of the administrative e-signatures certification system.

30. Restructuring Informatization Organizations and Personnel: This project was promoted to cope with new information environment changes such as information resource management, information protection, and NCIA establishment. Specifically, it was aimed at improving the information workforce and organizational structure within the government and strengthening its propelling capability. As NCIA was established and operated, the function and role of the organization were also determined. In addition, a plan to strengthen the capacity of the government-affiliated IT organization was prepared and a plan for strengthening education and training was established to improve professionalism. Specifically, in 2005, the Presidential Committee on Government Innovation and Decentralization (PCGID) organized and operated the Task Force for this project.
31. Reforming the Legal System for E-Government and Security: The development of related laws is a prerequisite for the successful implementation of e-government. The PCGID adopted a plan to consolidate legislation related to e-government and proposed the drawing up of a Privacy Act, identifying 775 laws and regulations to be examined. Out of a total of 775 legal institutions related to electronic processing of civil applications, laws and regulations have been examined by their responsible agencies, and related enforcement ordinances handled by MOGAHA. Taking into consideration the needs and urgency, law and regulations to be revised were identified; 379 regulations on 12 projects in 2004 and 450 regulations on 3 projects in 2005.

These 31 e-government projects continued to be implemented based on the roadmap for five years from 2003 to 2007. A total of 918 million US dollars was invested in these 31 projects for five years. These projects have been carried out through the implementation of numerous information systems and the basis for government innovation through systems were established. President Roh Moo-hyun attended the e-government completion ceremony on September 19, 2007 and declared that Korea's e-government base was completed and advanced and that it became a leading country in digital government.

PRESIDENT ROH MOO-HYUN'S E-GOVERNMENT LEADERSHIP ANALYSIS

The e-government policies promoted by the Roh Moo-hyun administration from 2003 to 2007 can be analyzed from the President's leadership perspective as follows. First of all, President Roh, unlike his predecessors or his successors, stressed the pursuit of e-government throughout the five years, starting from the early days of power. This was because the Roh Moo-hyun administration set the administrative agenda using information technology, that is, the promotion of e-government as the presidential agenda. In addition, a powerful e-Government governance body was established directly under the president. And he allocated substantial budget in e-government initiatives.

President's High Understanding of E-Government

President Roh Moo-hyun had excellent knowledge of ICT. In the past, when he operated a lawyer's office, he also showed his ability to develop an office operation management software program with PC. Therefore, he had a better understanding of the importance and use of ICT than any other previous president. President Roh Moo-hyun chose ICT as the most important means of government innovation, not merely as a technical or industrial product. Soon after his inauguration, he established the Government Innovation Decentralization Committee directly under the presidency and formed an e-government committee under it to promote e-government projects as a presidential project.

In this process, he also directly coordinated conflicts between ministries. He also held government innovation conferences and lecture workshops from time to time to improve the mindsets of senior government officials regarding digital government and government innovation. President Roh Moo-hyun pursued clean and transparent administration and anti-corruption prevention through e-government, as reflected in the following speech.

> "In the future, we will improve the way the public sector works, innovate business processes, and ... ... It is important to naturally change the functions and organization of government. In addition, active efforts should be made to ensure clean and transparent administration through e-government."
> 2003, 4, 17 National Agenda Meeting

> It is problem to raise transparency and integrity of administration. The implementation of e-government by Korea and the voluntary reform of public officials will be a driving force for a clean and transparent government. At the ninth meeting in 1999, Seoul's 'Online Procedures ENhancement for civil applications' was announced as an excellent case of anti-corruption. In addition, I and the Korean government will actively participate in international cooperation on anti-corruption and will cooperate with the activities of the Transparency International.
> 2003. 5. 26. Speech to the 11th International on Anti-Corruption Conference (IACC)

President Roh Moo-hyun's insights and intentions toward the electronic government were reflected in the e-government projects in Korea and Korea's electronic government policies achieved great results during the Roh Moo-hyun administration. When President Roh took office in 2003, UN e-government ranking of South Korea had remained outside the top 10; it improved to be ranked 5th by the end of his term in 2008 and soon achieved world's top place by 2010.

In fact, President Roh frequently expressed interest in UN e-government rankings during his service. During his presidency, he hoped for Korea to achieve top rank status in the UN e-Government evaluation. In particular, at that time, the UN e-government development stage consisted of five stages, and he ordered government officials to enter Korea in the fifth stage as soon as possible. With such strong interest of the president, Korea was able to rank high in the UN e-Government survey today.

E-Government Upgraded to Presidential Agenda

As we have seen, before the Roh Moo-hyun president in Korea, the promotion of the e-government was carried out on the presidential agenda even under Kim Dae-jung administration. This period, however, did not gain much momentum because it was the second half period of President Kim's term. On the contrary, President Roh strongly and systematically pushed for e-government policy as the presidential agenda from the early days of his administration.

In April 2003, to promote government innovation in a more comprehensive and systematic way, Roh Moo-hyun administration established the Presidential Committee on Government Innovation and Decentralization (PCGID) under the President and organized five professional committees to manage such major innovation projects as administrative reform, personnel administration system reform, decentralization, finance and tax systems reform, and the promotion of E-government.

The role of the e-government special committee of the Presidential Committee on Government Innovation and Decentralization (PCGID) at this time is described in a white paper by the Korean government (MOGAHA, 2006: 9-10).

> The Special Committee on e-Government under the PCGID carried out the development, deliberation, and coordination of the e-Government Roadmap projects during initial stages. The Ministry of Government Administration and Home Affairs (MOGAHA) provided administrative assistance while the National Information Society Agency (NIA) conducted project management along with technical advice. Each

government agency was assigned to perform and implement plans that were designed by the Committee.

With the necessity to strengthen the authority and position of the responsible ministry constantly being raised for efficient and responsible e-government implementation, the development, coordination, and management of e-government projects were performed by MOGAHA as the projects entered into full-scale implementation. The Special Committee on e-Government focused on advising and evaluating e-government projects.

Therefore, the implementation of e-government projects by the Roh Moo-hyun administration was carried out by the Presidential Committee on Government Innovation and Decentralization (PCGID). In this way, the promotion of e-government in the Roh Moo-hyun administration was pursued as a presidential agenda by the organization directly under the president. At the same time, a senior secretary position for innovation management, in charge of government innovation and e-government, was created in the Presidential office. Therefore, the Roh Moo-hyun administration pursued e-government policies in cooperation with the Presidential Office and the Special Committee on e-Government under the PCGID.

Using E-Government as the Most Powerful Means of Government Innovation

President Roh used e-government as the most powerful means of government innovation during his presidency. In particular, the Roh Moo-hyun government pursued the expansion of participatory democracy through electronic citizen participation since it aimed for a "participatory government."

The Roh Moo-hyun administration's 31 major e-government projects were carried out in connection with government innovation. In the Roh Moo-hyun administration, PCGID proclaimed the principle of promoting e-government roadmap projects in close connection with government innovation. To this end, a detailed action plan was prepared.

The Roh Moo-hyun administration's vision of administrative reform was set as a "government that works well with the people." The goals for achieving this were efficient administration, service-oriented administration, transparent administration, participatory administration, and clean administration. The specific agenda for achieving this goal can be summarized as follows (PCGID, 2007: 32-67).

1. Efficient Administration: The main tasks to build an efficient administration include the construction of a national evaluation infrastructure, the improvement of working methods through BPR (Business Process Reengineering), the establishment of a flexible organizational culture, the redesign of government organizations, and an emphasis on developing a horizontal policy coordination system.
2. Service-oriented Administration: Service is one of the basic duties of the government. Improvement of the administrative service transfer system and the establishment of a service-oriented system for civil appeals were suggested as major agenda items. The sub-tasks include the promotion of service standards, the improvement the system to contract out administrative service to private sectors, the construction of a nation-wide network for handling civil appeals and applications, an increase of adequate service provisions to the socially underprivileged, and an improvement of the management of neglected civil appeals.
3. Transparent Administration: Securing transparency is an important prerequisite for earning trust from the public. To improve government transparency, active openness and higher transparency in administrative activities were suggested as key elements of the agenda. Specific tasks also include the expansion of disclosure and access to administrative information, the enhancement of transparency in administrative procedure, transparency in decision making, and the expansion of Internet civil affairs services.

4. Participatory Administration: As the word participatory implies, national governance is the proper task not only of government also but also through the cooperation and interaction between the government and civil society. The agenda for participatory administration are the enforcement of cooperative governance with civil society and active support for public service. Specific tasks include actively maintaining a policy community, adopting the professional Ombudsman System, establishing the People's Survey and infrastructure for volunteer activities, and improving conditions for civic group activities.
5. Clean (Ethical) Administration: Throughout the history of the Korean government, much emphasis has been placed on maintaining clean administration by eliminating corruption among public officials. The Participatory Government is no exception. It has put the systematic response to corruption and the promotion of a higher sense of ethics among public officials as priorities on its agenda. Specific tasks proposed include improving the systems and regulations that induce irregularity, devising anti-corruption measures for each sector, imposing checks and balances among inspection institutions, focusing on the substance of action plans, improving public ethics, and eliminating the authoritative administrative culture.

All these national agendas were promoted as part of the e-government project. In order for President Roh to directly manage these national agenda, national agenda meetings were held weekly or biweekly. At this meeting, President Roh Moo-hyun always emphasized government innovation, transparent government, and e-government. As such, the promotion of the e-government was the president's agenda mentioned by the President every week in the Roh Moo-hyun government and was recognized as the most important means of government innovation.

In this regard, it is noteworthy that the president was dedicated to establishing an e-government system. President Roh not only developed the government business management system but also attempted its rapid establishment. He encouraged the use of the system by all central ministries, commented directly on employee reports, and encouraged the use of public officials. In particular, in order to utilize the e-government system, on July 14, 2006 and February 28, 2007, the government held two learning sessions with ministers and deputy ministers of each ministry where the President himself explained how to use the system (MOPAS, 2016). In this process, the president directly emphasized the improvement of the utilization of the work management system in all ministries. The president-led ministers' e-government learning workshops can be said to have contributed greatly to the utilization of the e-government system.

As e-government policy emerged as a major national agenda in the Roh Moo-hyun administration, the Ministry of Information and Communication (MIC) and the Ministry of Government Administration and Home Affairs (MOGAHA) competed with each other to secure the initiative in e-government projects. Since the MIC held a far superior position in terms of department size and budget, PCGID's Special Committee on E-Government were unable to respond appropriately to this issue. Finally, in February 2006, President Roh Moo-hyun coordinated the role between the two ministries at the National Agenda Meeting. As a result, the Ministry of Government Affairs and Home Affairs, which is in charge of government innovation, was dedicated to e-government, and the Ministry of Information and Communication became responsible for promoting related infrastructure.

However, these examples do not necessarily show President Roh's leadership in e-government. As can be seen from the Clinton administration in the US case, the e-government leadership is not about the President's direct engagement but rather involves selecting and trasnferring authority to the right people. From this point of view, the case of Roh's direct adjustment of ministries' roles at that time alone would not be considered as a success factor.

Significant Increase in E-Government Project Budget

Korea's establishment of world-class infrastructure in the telecommunications sector over the past two decades is due to the proper use of the Information Promotion Fund. In the 1980s, Korea pursued a national basic information system project and used an "Investment First, Settlement Later" budget system (MOIS, 2017b: 20). Furthermore, Korea has achieved dramatic results in the expansion of budgetary investment in the promotion of e-government. The contents of budget investment in ICT field and budget increase of e-government projects in the Roh Moo-hyun government are as follows.

Korea's budget consists of general accounting, special accounting, and fund. Until 2003, general accounting was used among the information promotion funds started in 1995. Therefore, the 11 projects of the Kim Dae-jung administration's e-government were funded by the information promotion fund. Subsequently, the Roh Moo-hyun administration's 31 major e-government projects were transferred from the ICT Promotion Fund of the MIC to the e-government budget and the general account of the MOGAHA.

During the period from 2003 to 2007, a total budget of USD 981 million was invested in e-government implementation as shown in Table 6.

Table 6. Budget for the e-Government roadmap 31 Initiatives (Unit: USD million)

Year	2003	2004	2005	2006	2007	Total
Budget	23.4	111	220.2	275.7	287.7	918

Source: MOGAHA, 2006: 10.

In 2003, 31 projects were selected but the budget spent was relatively small, mainly due to information strategy planning (ISP) and business process reengineering (BPR). Since 2004, 31 major e-government projects began operation and the budgets were implemented. This trend continued from 2005 to 2007 (MOPAS, 2008).

However, after the launch of a new government in 2008, the overall budget for e-government began to shrink sharply. The above table is limited to the 31 e-government projects of the Roh Moo-hyun administration, but this is expanded to e-government support projects of all ministries organized by MOGAHA and displayed by year as shown in Table 7. This is a budget trend for the past decade of e-government projects in several ministries that are supported by the MOGAHA.

**Table 7. Budget for the e-Government Support Project
(Unit: USD million)**

Year	2005	2006	2007	2008	2009	2010	2011	2012	2013	2014	2015
Budget	220	275	287	143	130	160	130	108	58	83	126

Since 2008, when the Roh Moo-hyun administration's 31 major e-government projects were completed, investment in e-government in Korea has rapidly curtailed. In 2008, the first year of the Lee Myung-bak administration, the budget was reduced by half compared to the previous year. The reduction trend continued in the Park Geun-hye administration. In 2013, the early days of the Park Geun-hye administration, investments in e-government support projects decreased significantly compared to the previous year as ISP-driven projects were pursued due to the necessity of promoting projects linked with new government agendas. The decline was also large, allocating a budget of $ 58 million in 2013 which was only 54% of the $ 108 million in 2012.

This is all due to the change in presidency and the launch of a new administration. In other words, the budget invested by the e-government varies greatly depending on the president's interest in e-government. As such, Korea has experienced a "lost decade" in the field of e-government over the past decade. Over the past decade, South Korea's e-government systems have failed to advance and have become obsolete. This can be seen from the fact that the e-government systems built by the Roh Moo-hyun administration have been consistently used and maintained over the last decade.

Now, starting in 2019, South Korea is embarking on a new digital innovation and intelligent information age to upgrade existing aging e-government systems.

CASE STUDY: THE STORY OF THE PRESIDENT HIMSELF DEVELOPING THE E-GOVERNMENT SYSTEM

On March 12, 2004, due to Roh's "political neutrality," the opposition parties in South Korea's National Assembly decided to impeach the president and resulted in 193 voted in favor of impeachment and two votes in opposition. As a result, President Roh's duties were suspended and the Prime Minister acted on behalf of the President. On May 14, 2004, the impeachment proposal was rejected by the Constitutional Court and President Roh returned to office 64 days after his prosecution.

This impeachment of President Roh Moo-hyun left an episode regarding the development of the e-government system in Korea. This involved the development of "e-support," the President's Office (Blue House) business process management system (BH-BPS). In April 2004, President Roh was unable to engage in politics and administrative affairs and chose to develop a President Office business process management system that he knew well. During the impeachment period, President Roh sought to develop and spread the Blue House business process management system (BH-BPS).

President Roh Moo-hyun directly participated in the BH-BPS development team as a developer, to design document management and task management processes with experts. In addition, for the early settlement of BH-BPS, President Roh mandated that all reports went through the BH-BPS. In addition, President Roh was passionate about holding learning sessions and the president himself volunteered as a change management education instructor.

Subsequently, in the summer of 2004, he instructed to develop a government business process management system (On-Nara BPS) that would revolutionize the way the government works, based on the BH BPS he developed. Based on this order, the BPR/ISP project was implemented from August to November 2004 to establish the On-Nara BPS. In February 2005, the Integrated Administration and Innovation Promotion Team was formed in the Ministry of Government Administration and Home Affairs (MOGAHA).

The purpose of On-Nara BPS includes standardization of the entire administrative process, scientific and systematic process management, sharing of knowledge information, and linkage of work assignments (MOPAS, 2016). First, it aims to standardize the entire administrative process through the information system. Second, it intends to classify decentralized and complicated government business processes by function and unit assignment and systematically manage them, from the planning stage to execution. Third, various processes are linked and integrated to assist with the sharing of knowledge information based on the system.

On-nara BPS not only contributes to enhancing achievements of each administrative institution, but it also supports national affairs management by organically connecting to other governmental systems. It links and integrates the achievements management systems of each institution to effectively manage the execution of important national projects. As a result, On-nara BPS discloses the progress of national projects and its achievements to the general public in order to enhance transparency in national affairs management and improve governmental accountability.

The On-Nara BPS was first adopted by the MOGAHA in early 2005 and then spread to 48 central ministries by the end of 2006, after a pilot test of five central administrative agencies until spring 2006. As of the end of 2018, the On-Nara BPS in Korea is being used by 630,000 officials in 289 central and local governments. South Korean officials work online every day through document management and memo reporting through the On-Nara BPS. As such, the On-Nara BPS plays a pivotal role in administration by being closely linked and integrated with related systems such as performance management and government business evaluation.

The fact that the president of a country directly participated in the development of the government's business process management system and spread it would be a rare case in the world. This was possible because Roh was familiar with using ICT such as developing a lawyer's office work program using the PC version of dBaseIII Macro. It was also possible because such skills were combined with the president's willingness to innovate the government to change the way government worked and to support transparent administrative processes. Therefore, the Republic of Korea is still indebted to President Roh Moo-hyun for its success in e-government to this day.

CONCLUSION: LESSONS LEARNED

The promotion of e-government started in earnest in Korea since the Kim Dae-jung administration in 2000. Later, in the Roh Moo-hyun administration in 2003, the e-government was systematically promoted from the early days as the presidential agenda. Based on this, Korea ranked first in the world three times in a row in the UN e-Government evaluation in 2010, 2012, and 2014. This was possible because South Korea had President Roh as its leader. Based on the background of President Roh Moo-hyun's term, three lessons can be summarized as follows.

Political Aspects of E-Government Policy

In the Roh Moo-hyun administration, e-government projects were strongly promoted as the presidential agenda. Therefore, from 2003 to 2007, the president tried to complete all 31 of the e-government projects during his term. In addition, in December 2007, $ 300,000 was spent in establishing the next-generation e-government vision and strategy (MOGAHA, 2007). This was the basic plan for the development of e-government in Korea after 2008.

However, the Lee Myung-bak administration, which was launched in February 2008, negated Roh's plans. It also banned the use of the term "e-government." In the Lee Myung-bak administration, the term of "e-government" was replaced by the word "national informatization." Subsequently, budgets allocated to e-government projects were also cut by more than 30%, which was allocated to other government agendas. The e-government term, which was banned, was allowed to be used after the 2010 UN evaluation. The e-government ceremony has been held every year since the government's replacement in 2017.

The Korean government celebrated the 50th anniversary of the e-government on November 1, 2017. At this ceremony conference, the Korean government awarded 30 people, 10 services, 10 companies and organizations that contributed to the development of Korean e-government. In commemoration of the 50th anniversary of the e-government, the Korean government revised the e-government law to enact the e-government day. The e-government day established by the Korean government is June 24. Therefore, since 2018, Korea has designated June 24 as the e-government day and has been celebrating it through government-led ceremonies every year.

This means that e-government policy is not about simply introducing information technology or developing information systems in administration. E-government is essentially a government innovation using information technology and a holistic governmental reform. Therefore, it can be regarded as a highly political action of government in this respect. Therefore, e-government can be successfully pursued only if it's based on the president's will and leadership. But there is a dilemma here. Eventually the president is replaced and the new government takes office, so it is important to ensure the permanence of the e-government policy. In this case, it is necessary to designate a national CIO and institutionalize it and not rely on the ability of the president's own leadership.

Time Lag Effect of E-Government Policy: Elimination of Short-Term Achievements

In January 2010, when the United Nations published the results of evaluating Korea as the No. 1 nation in e-government, the Lee Myung-bak administration released the following press release.

> According to the recently announced 2010 UN e-Government Servey, the UN announced that Korea has achieved the world's No. 1 ranking in both the E-Government Preparation Index and the Online Participation Index. This is because the Lee Myung-bak administration's national informatization policy has achieved tangible results over the past two years. In addition, there has been an opportunity for Korea's national informatization to take off again, disregarding the concerns of informatization and IT neglect. (Omitted Below......)
>
> This achievement is interpreted to have gained momentum for Korea to lead the global e-government in the future. The evaluation results were largely driven by policy efforts such as the Lee Myung-bak administration's national informatization vision, strategy establishment, full revision of the National Informatization Basic Act, and the establishment of a control tower. (Omitted Below......)
> Source: MOSPA, 2010: Jan 15, Press Release.

However, the content of this press release, distributed by the Korean government at the time, is far from the truth. The reason why Korea ranked first in the UN's e-government evaluation in 2010 was not because of the Lee Myung-bak administration's national informatization policy but because of the Roh Moo-hyun administration's 31 e-government projects. As a result of the e-government projects implemented from 2003 to 2007, the utilization of e-government systems in Korea began to increase from 2008. In early 2009, the Korean government selected 10 of the 31 e-government projects and translated the contents and their utilization into English and submitted them to the UN. At that time, the United Nations ranked Korea as the world's number one e-government based on the results of the Roh Moo-hyun administration's 31 e-government projects.

An important aspect here is the time lag effect of the e-government policy. In other words, e-government projects and policies are not carried out in a short time. Especially after the system is introduced, much time and effort are required for activation and upgrading. In addition, disagreements among ministries may lead to delays or failures in the process of building such information systems. Of the 31 e-government projects in Korea, two projects were delayed by two to three years due to conflicts between ministries in the process. Thus, Korea's first place in the UN e-government evaluation in January 2010 is not the achievement of the Lee Myung-bak administration but the result of the Roh Moo-hyun administration's e-government policy.

Institutional Foundation: Need to Designate a National CIO and Secure a Budget

Although this article emphasized the role of the president in the promotion of the Korean e-government, this is a rare case in other countries. In general, what is more important in the promotion of e-government is the establishment of an institutional basis that can consistently plan and implement the policies. The most important of these institutional foundations are people and budgets.

President Roh had excellent insights in the field of e-government, participated in the development of e-government system directly, and always emphasized the importance of e-government to all the ministers. These actions may be highly commended as good examples of the president's leadership. In practice, however, presidential leadership does not mean that the president does it all by himself.

It is important for the president to transfer the power of e-government to experts, just as the U.S. President Bill Clinton handed over the power of innovation and informatization to the Vice President Al Gore to lead the NPR in 1993 (NPR, 1997). In this case, an expert who can combine ICT and administrative innovation should be identified and designated as a national CIO. And it is important for the president to give the national CIO full control over government innovation, including e-government or latest digital transformation-related policies. In this process, ICT governance must be properly designed and relevant organizations should be empowered.

Along with this, another important consideration is the budget allocation. In the case of Korea, e-government policies have been continuously implemented for the past 20 years through the information promotion fund and e-government support project budgets. Therefore, considering that budget is the most powerful means of control, in order to implement e-government and digital government, it is necessary to devise a stable budget to raise the policy priority. Since e-government is evolving into an intelligent government in many countries, including Korea today, an institutional foundation must be established to support it (MOIS, 2017a).

ACKNOWLEDGMENTS

This work was supported by the National Research Foundation of Korea Grant funded by the Korean Government (NRF-2017S1A3A2066084).

REFERENCES

Accenture. (2001). *eGovernment Leadership: Rhetoric vs Reality -Closing the Gap*. Washington, DC, July 2001.

Ahn, Michael. (2017). Critical Factors behind Korean E-Government Success: A Conversation with the Chairman of Korea's Presidential Special Committee of EGovernment. Chen, Y. C. & Ahn, M. *Routledge Handbook on Information Technology in Government*. New York: Routledge.

Caldow, Janet. (1999). *The Quest for Electronic Government: A Defining Vision.* Washington D.C.: Institute for Electronic Government IBM Corporation. July, 1999.

Chung, Choong-Sik. (1997). *A Study on the Critical Success Factors for thr Electronic Government Realization.* PhD Dissertation. Seoul: Sungkyunkwan University. Republic of Korea.

Chung, Choong-Sik. (2015). "The Introduction of e-Government in Korea: Development Journey, Outcomes and Future," *Gestion et management public*, 2015/2 (Volume 3/n 4), p. 107-122. France. doi 10.3917/gmp.034.0107.

Chung, Choong-Sik. (2019). Analysis on the 2018 UN E-Government Survey. *Journal of Advanced Research in Dynamical and Control Systems,* 11(7-S), 1242-1252.

Chung, Choong-Sik & Kim, Sung-Bou. (2019). "A Comparative Study of Digital Government Policies: Focusing on E-Government Acts in Korea and the United States," *Electronics* 2019, 8, 1362.

Deloitte Research. (2000). *At the dawn of e-Government: The citizen as customer.* Pittsburgh, PA. USA.

Kamensky, M. John. (1996). Role of the "Reinventing Government" Movement in Federal Management Reform, *Public Administration Review.* 56(3): 247-255.

Ministry of the Interior and Safety (MOIS). (2017a). *Intelligent Government Basic Plan*, March, 2017. Korea.

Ministry of the Interior and Safety (MOIS). (2017b). *50 Years Footprints of Korean e-Government 1967-2017.* October, 2017. Korea.

Ministry of Government Administration and Home Affairs. (MOGAHA). (2006). *2006 Annual Report for e-Government.* December 30. Seoul: Republic of Korea.

Ministry of Government Administration and Home Affairs. (MOGAHA). (2007). *Master Plan for the Next Generation e-Government in Korea.* December, 2007. Seoul: Republic of Korea.

Ministry of Safety and Public Administration. (MOSPA). (2010). Press Release. *Achieved the world's No. 1 ranking in UN e-Government in 2010*, Jan 15, 2010. Seoul: Republic of Korea.

Ministry of Public Administration and Security. (MOPAS). (2008). *2003-2007 E-Government Project White Paper*. June, 30. Seoul: Republic of Korea.

Ministry of Public Administration and Security. (MOPAS). (2016). *On-nara BPS*. Seoul: Republic of Korea.

NPR. (1993). *Reengineering Through Information Technology*. Washington, D.C.: U.S. Government Printing Office.

NPR. (1997). *Access America: Reengineering Through Information Technology*. Washington, D.C.: U.S. Government Printing Office.

OECD. (2003). *OECD E-Government Studies: The E-Government Imperative*. Paris: OECD Publishing.

Presidential Committee on Government Innovation & Decentralization. (PCGID). (2007). *Innovation & Decentralization of Korean Government: 2003-2007*. Republic of Korea.

Song, Hee joon. (2002). Prospects and Limitations of the E-Government Initiative in Korea. *International Review of Public Administration*. 7(2): 45-53. KAPA, Seoul, Korea.

Song, Hee-joon and Cho, Tak. (2007). "Electronic Government of Korea - Performance and Tasks," *Informatization Policy*, Vol. 14, No. 4, pp. 20-37.

Special Committee for e-Government (SCEG). (2003). *Korea's e-Government: Completion of e-Government Framework*. Republic of Korea. January 2003.

United Nations. (2010). *UN E-Government Survey 2010: Leveraging e-Government at a time of Financial and Economic Crisis*. New York: United Nations Publication.

United Nations. (2012). *UN E-Government Survey 2012: E-Government for the People*. New York: United Nations Publication.

United Nations. (2014). *UN E-Government Survey 2014: E-Government for the Future We Want*. New York: United Nations Publication.

United Nations. (2018). *UN E-Government Survey 2018: Gearing e-Government to Support Transformation towards Sustainable and Resilient Societies*. New York: United Nations Publication.

In: e-Government
Editor: Anil Sieben

ISBN: 978-1-53617-563-9
© 2020 Nova Science Publishers, Inc.

Chapter 5

DETERMINANTS OF CITIZENS' E-GOVERNMENT ADOPTION SERVICES IN GREECE

Anastasia Voutinioti[*]
Department of Business and Organizations Administration,
University of the Peloponnese, Kalamata, Greece

ABSTRACT

This research aimed to investigate citizens' behavior and the role of the 'Citizen Service Centers' (CSCs) in e-government adoption in Greece. The ultimate aim was to contribute to the understanding of the user's intention drivers or barriers in the e-government take-up, building a theory, and proposing a validation research framework. It validated the UTAUT2 model in the Greek context, by using a quantitative research approach, focusing on the CSCs that act as intermediaries. The SEM validation of the proposed model revealed that 'performance expectancy', 'trust in the government', 'trust in the Internet', and 'effort expectancy' were vital drivers that positively influenced the users' intentions. The 'habit of going to CSCs' was negatively related to users' intentions. This

---
[*] Corresponding Author's E-mail: avoutinioti@teikal.gr.

meant that the way CSCs operate did not help in e-government take-up. At the practical level, the research provided e-government policymakers and web designers with practical recommendations to better plan, design, and implement policies to increase the e-government take-up.

Keywords: e-government, e-government adoption, UTAUT2, citizen service centers, Greece

1. INTRODUCTION

Many governments around the world have launched e-government initiatives because of the many benefits, e.g., better governance, more convenient ways of information, and service delivery (Al-Sobhi 2011). A significant amount of resources have been spent on e-government projects, and their expected success is high. Nevertheless, many e-government projects fail for different reasons. Researchers argued that the success of e-government initiatives is dependent on government support but also on citizens' willingness to accept and adopt those e-government services (Warkentin et al. 2002). Without citizens' acceptability and adoption, such initiatives could not achieve their intended goals. They also made the point that, although there is enormous potential for online government services, citizens are not adopting those (Warkentin et al. 2002). In some countries, e.g., Greece, little attention has been given to the citizens' perspective. Even less research has been conducted at the local government context (Carter and Weerakkody 2008) despite that, it is suggested to evaluate e-government acceptance at the local government level (Fan 2015).

This chapter highlights factors that facilitate or impede Greeks in using e-services and examines the roles of the Citizen Service Centers (CSCs) that operate in Greece. Its purpose is to build a model for identifying the factors that mostly affect citizens' intention to use e-government services; to develop an instrument (i.e., questionnaire) for assessing citizens' intention to use the e-services and to provide concrete managerial implications for practitioners.

The remainder of the chapter is organized as follows. In section 2, the e-government in Greece is presented, while in section 3, the essential models in e-government adoption are mentioned. Accurately, the UTAUT2 used in this study is described in addition to other factors that extended it. In section 4, the proposed model and the methodology of the study are presented. In sections 5 and 6, the results are reported and discussed, while in section 7, the implications for policymakers are given.

2. E-GOVERNMENT IN GREECE

Several initiatives have been implemented by the Greek government to assist in ICT and e-government diffusion. In the late 1990s, the Greek government agencies initiated their web presence. In 2002, the national e-government agenda included the establishment of the CSCs, to accomplish the 'one-stop government' strategy. They have been operating all over the country under the local government agencies. In 2011, the reform program 'Kallikratis' led to consolidation into fewer and larger municipalities (http://kallikratis.ypes.gr/). Then new CSCs were established in the old municipal structures to lessen the perception of the loss of proximity that occurred when local entities increased in size. The main reasons CSCs were introduced to Greek e-government strategy was to set up a link between government and citizens, provide more convenient ways in the delivery of services and assist ICT inexperienced citizens in adopting e-government systems. Another reason was to overcome the difficulty of verifying the identity of citizens, as up to now, there are limited e-identification and e-signature provision in Greece. Other reasons included issues such as low level of trust in government and e-services, information privacy, and security concerns (Voutinioti 2014b). Although self-access of e-services in CSCs, was a fundamental principle, up to now is not available due to their limited resources and capabilities. They mostly provide face-to-face contact with citizens, perform services on citizens' behalf, and control the transactions flow between government and citizens, in both directions. They comprise a governmental multi-service facility, and so far, they have enjoyed citizens' trust (Voutinioti 2014b). They are gradually transformed into e-CSCs, following government legislation and technical requirements in terms of security, data protection, and electronic transactions. Their webpage (www.kep.gov.gr), providing information on government services, does not have much traffic. As far as government websites are concerned, they have been mainly evolved to valuable information, and their traffic is low too. The same implies to local government webpages (Voutinioti 2014b).

Although the Greek government has invested heavily in e-government implementation, there have been varying results and delayed outcomes. Digital public services remain one of the most challenging areas of the digital economy and society. Greece is making progress, but its performance is well below the EU average, and it ranks last of the 28 Member States. eGovernment users stood at 38% (EU average 58%). In the provision of online public services, Greece made some progress in 2017, with 14% pre-filled forms, but it remained far below the EU average of 53%, ranking 27th (European Commission, Digital Economy, and Society Index 2018). The e-government service users were 38%, while the EU average was 58%. Also, Greeks (81%) do not trust the government and local government (Eurobarometer 90 2018). All the above, strongly suggest that Greece needs to increase its efforts to get into the e-government era and to encourage citizens to use the e-services.

3. LITERATURE REVIEW

The E-Government Adoption Models

There are numerous theories and models developed and reported in the literature that explain the individual intention and usage of the e-government services, with the TAM, TPB, DOI, UTAUT, and UTAUT2 being the most important (Rana, Dwivedi and Williams 2013). First, the TAM has received extensive support for predicting the use of Information Systems (IS) and is considered the most influential model in explaining adoption behavior (Gefen et al. 2003). Nevertheless, TAM excludes some relevant sources of variance and does not consider issues, e.g., social influence or other conditions that would enable an individual to use an IS. The TPB model (Taylor and Todd 1995) extends the TAM by inserting the factor 'perceived behavioral control'. This model delivers more specific information, e.g., factors that might be barriers to system use. The DOI model (Rogers 2003), was designed to analyze the characteristics of technology adopters. It is mostly applied to the adoption of technology for performing job roles, and it may not be as valid when applied to consumers. In an extensive literature review of e-government adoption, Rana, Dwivedi, and Williams (2013), concluded that none of these two later models was well utilized.

In 2003, a new model was developed, the Unified Theory of Acceptance and Use of Technology (UTAUT) (Venkatesh et al. 2003), to predict intention (INT) and usage of new technology. It combined factors of eight previous theoretical models and is made up of three key factors, determinants of INT: (1) 'Performance expectancy' (PE), the belief of an individual whether the technology helps to boost performance. (2) 'Effort expectancy' (EE), the perceived degree of effort that the existing technical and organizational infrastructure is suited to use technology (3) 'Social influence' (SI), the perception of an individual that others think she/he should use the technology. The fourth factor 'facilitating conditions' (FC), whether the individual believes that the existing technical and organizational infrastructure is suited to use the technology, affected 'usage behavior.' UTAUT also posits the role of four key moderator variables (age, gender, experience, and voluntariness of use). The model improved the explained variance of technology acceptance to 70% over the previous models, which explained about 40% (Venkatesh et al. 2003). According to Rana, Dwivedi, and Williams (2013), it has been extensively tested and cross-validated using different technologies in organizations and mandatory and voluntary settings. Hence, it is considered enhanced, parsimonious with robust characteristics that could better explain the individual's INT and 'usage'.

Venkatesh et al. (2012), developed the UTAUT2 model, which examined the consumer acceptance of the technology. It was developed and empirically tested to determine the INT and 'use behavior' of watching mobile videos and playing online games. By changing the context (from organizational to consumer), the old constructs and relationships remained, but new ones got introduced: (1) 'Hedonic motivation', the perceived enjoyment of using a particular technology, i.e., music, games, and entertainment. These hedonic features do not apply to the government websites, as they cover practical aspects of the web services. Hence, 'hedonic motivation' is irrelevant in the context of this study. (2) 'Price value', the cognitive tradeoff between the perceived benefits of the applications and the monetary cost of using those. As e-government services do not include any price or fee, it is irrelevant too. Thus, these two factors got excluded. (3) The third new factor, 'habit' is defined as 'the extent to which people tend to perform behaviors automatically because of learning' (Venkatesh et al. 2012, 161). Venkatesh et al. (2012) found 'habit' to be a key driver of INT. In this study, it is important to consider 'habit' because: (a) citizens by intending to adopt e-government services, the 'new behavior' competes with the 'incumbent behavior' to personally go to local government agencies or CSCs. (b) The habitual patterns can explain citizens' resistance to use e-services. Therefore the inhibiting effect of 'habit' should be taken into account. However, in this case, there is no habit established because e-services are of little use (Voutinioti 2014b). Hence, it is impossible to measure 'habit' for initial users. Nevertheless, Greeks are used to go to CSCs to get serviced and have already formed a 'habit of using CSCs' (HBC). Hence, HBC and the possible effects on the INT of using e-services can be examined.

Susanto and Goodwin (2013), argued that the results from many studies pointed out that the seven variables in UTAUT2 captured about 42 different variables used in all previous adoption theories. These variables influenced directly or indirectly consumer 'intention' and 'use' in various contexts, e.g., e-government. These concepts seemed appropriate in approaching the aims of this study. Nevertheless, there were remaining determinants not fully explored for the Greek context, because of the dominant national culture, the level of use and interaction, and commitment to the e-government initiatives. Thus an extended UTAUT2 model with additional factors was needed.

Additional Factors

Research of online behavior emphasized the importance of including 'trust' in adoption models to gain a more comprehensive understanding of user acceptance of e-services and to improve the explanatory power of the models (Belanger and Carter 2008; Voutinioti 2014a; Fakhoury and Baker 2016). Trust is a critical enabler in impersonal situations with a level of uncertainty, like online environments. On contrast, lack of trust is one of the most critical barriers to e-service adoption, where personal or financial information is involved (Belanger and Carter 2008). In literature, there is a distinction between types of trust (Gefen et al. 2003; Belanger and Carter 2008): (a) 'Trust in the Government' (TOG) that refers to trust in the government institution providing the e-service. TOG is defined as 'one's perceptions regarding the integrity and ability of the agency providing the service' (Belanger and Carter 2008, 167). Candid, non-fraudulent interaction with e-service providers will enhance citizen trust and acceptance of e-services. On the contrary, dishonesty from government officials and employees will decrease trust and engagement in these initiatives (Belanger and Carter 2008). TOG also depends on the citizens' perceptions that these organizations have the will and possess the technical resources necessary to implement and secure e-services (Belanger and Carter 2008). This factor is of crucial importance for the Greeks because they do not trust the government and local government organizations. (b) 'Trust in the internet' (TOI), is defined as 'an individual's perceptions of the institutional environment, including the structures and regulations that make an environment feel safe' (Belanger and Carter 2008, 167). The Internet is still a source of uncertainty, especially for some countries, and the citizens' lack of trust in the Internet is a barrier to their adoption of e-services (Fakhoury and Baker 2016). In this study, a new trust factor was introduced, 'trust in the CSCs' (TOC), and is defined similarly to TOG, as CSCs are government agencies. In literature, it is acknowledged that CSCs, being the intermediaries of government, are widely accepted and enjoy peoples' trust (Al-Sobhi 2011). Trust in the intermediaries enhances trust in e-government services since citizens provide their personal information to the government portals via an authorized third party. Trust in e-government, in turn, enhances citizens' intention to use e-services (Al-Sobhi 2011).

This study also investigated the impact of demographics and the Uncertainty Avoidance (UA) cultural variable, as moderators to the INT. Researchers in e-government are usually investigating the role of demographics such as gender, age, educational level, prior experience, and income. Besides, the Hofstede's cultural variable UA has been found in the literature, to be a robust negative determinant of the intentions to use e-services (Cabinakova et al. 2013; Al-Hujran et al. 2011). It is also much of importance for the Greeks because, according to Hofstede (2011), they have a perfect score of 100 in UA. Greeks perceive electronic services as threatening because they are new to them and involve risks. Hence, the demographics and UA were examined as exogenous variables, and their effects on INT were assessed.

4. THE RESEARCH

The Proposed Model and Hypotheses

This study, following a quantitative approach, used a survey to understand citizens' perspectives regarding e-government adoption. A conceptual model was established by extending the UTAUT2 model with the TOG, TOI, and TOC factors. An instrument (questionnaire) was created to validate the proposed model empirically. The items of the questionnaire were partly based on UTAUT2, the rest (i.e., 'TOG, TOI, TOC) were adopted from Carter and Belanger (2005), and two items in the HBC factor were adapted from Al-Sobhi (2011). They have been reworked to suit the context of the study. Intention captured the motivational factors that drive a person to perform a behavior (Ajzen 1991). Intentions have been extensively reported to be a strong predictor of actual use (Ajzen 1991; Venkatesh et al. 2003). Hence, this relationship was omitted. All the constructs in the proposed model and the relations among them are depicted in Figure 1.

Then the following hypotheses were proposed, based primarily on Venkatesh et al., (2012) findings.

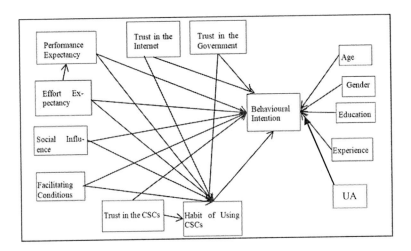

Figure 1. The proposed model in SEM notation.

H1: PE will positively affect INT	H16: Age will positively affect INT
H2: EE will positively affect INT	H17: Males will positively affect INT
H3: EE will positively affect PE	H H18: Education will positively affect INT
H4: SI will positively affect INT	H19: Experience will positively affect INT
H5: FC will positively affect INT	H20: Uncertainty Avoidance will negatively affect INT
H6: HBC will negatively affect INT	
H7: PE will negatively affect HBC	
H8: EE will negatively affect HBC	
H9: FC will negatively affect HBC	
H10: TOG will positively affect INT	
H11: TOG will negatively affect HBC	
H12: TOI will positively affect INT	
H13: TOI will negatively affect HBC	
H14: TOC will positively affect HBC	
H15: TOC will positively affect INT	

Conducting the Survey

First, a questionnaire in English was created that was reviewed for content validity by a group of IS academics. The questionnaire had to be administered in Greek to approximate the level of understanding of the respondents. Hence the questionnaire items were translated into Greek and then back to English to ensure translation equivalence (back-translation). The questions of all factors' measures used in the questionnaire were of 7 Likert-type scales. They were drawn from previous research where they were reported valid and reliable measures to the factors they were supposed to measure. Nevertheless, because of the translation, they had to be assessed again.

The final Greek version of the questionnaire was pretested to a convenience sample of 49 students of the University of the Peloponnese[1], Athens, or Heraklion city residents to verify its appropriateness and comprehensiveness. Cronbach's alpha was used to test the instrument's reliability. This sample was not included in the final survey. The test revealed that the questionnaire had to be altered to eliminate misunderstandings. After the amendments, it consisted of 9 factors and 35 items.

The final data came from two city citizens. The criteria used for selecting the appropriate municipalities called for the cases that provided e-services in the higher stages of e-government maturity. First, the cases representing successful municipalities in e-government implementation were identified. Among them, the cities of Athens, Heraklion (Southern Greece) and Thessaloniki in the North, were chosen. The criterion was the provision of transactional services. Researchers that reviewed different e-government stage models argued that the transaction stage is a critical one (Al-Sebie 2014). This stage enables two-way communication, and as a result, citizens can conduct complete transactions online, which enhances the interactivity among government and citizens and helps in reducing both costs and time. This criterion was met by the two municipalities of Athens

---

[1] Former Technological Educational Institute of the Peloponnese.

and Heraklion; Thessaloniki did not offer transactional services at the time of the survey. Afterward, the municipalities' website traffic was examined. According to www.alexa.com traffic statistics, all three webpages were the most broadly utilized among the other municipal webpages. Athens, Thessaloniki, and Heraklion were also the three Greek cities that were deemed 'smart cities of Europe' (ITRE, 2014), among 468 cities with a population of at least 100,000. All three were mentioned smart in at least three of the six axes. Only Athens and Heraklion cities were mentioned as smart in the 'Governance', and 'People', axes that were of the research's interest. Thus the selection was narrowed down to these two cities. Heraklion city is a medium city in population terms in the Crete region. Over the last years, Heraklion city has operated different e-government projects. The other municipality selected was the Athens city, the capital of Greece with a population of 540,000 habitants. This was the rationale for selecting these two cities to be used in the experiment.

The selected sampling method was convenience sampling (i.e., non-probability). An electronic survey was created, and officials from the two municipalities agreed to put the questionnaire on their webpage. All participants were Athens or Heraklion city citizens, familiar with the internet and CSCs' users. An email notifying for the survey with a link to the appropriate webpage providing the questionnaire was sent to different groups, to access a large number of participants. To alumni of the University of the Peloponnese, to different government and non-government employees, as well as to faculty and staff of the Universities located in these cities. It was also sent to local government blogposts and newsgroups, to the voluntary agencies operated in the two cities. To enable as much representation as possible, the use of multiple groups was necessary. To eliminate multiple responses by the same person, all respondents had to sign up on their municipal webpage and provide their username at the end of the questionnaire. The questionnaire also collected demographic data and data concerning participants' internet and e-government experience. All respondents were familiar with their respective websites since a familiarization task was involved. The instrument was administered for five weeks, and a total of 843 valid responses were returned. Generally, the large sample size was necessary because of the analysis (Structural Equation Modelling-SEM and the AMOS tool). For AMOS, the sample size should be at least ten times the largest number of independent constructs affecting a dependent construct, with a recommended minimum of 45 (Byrne 2010).

Data Analysis

The collected data were imported into SPSS statistical package, where a screening process took place. As the instrument was electronic, there were no missing values, nor outliers. Then the demographic analysis was carried out. The results are shown in Table 1.

In both samples, the respondents were younger, more educated, and ICT experienced than the average Greek population. They used the internet mostly for informational purposes and less for conducting transactions.

The primary analysis was conducted via AMOS. It included the Exploratory Factor Analysis (EFA), the Confirmatory Factor Analysis (CFA) and the structural model analysis. The EFA was carried out via SPSS to determine the appropriateness of the sample for factor analysis, the number of factors and assess the reliability of the factors. Within the CFA using AMOS, i.e., the measurement model analysis, the goodness of fit indices (GOF) were inspected, and the validity of each factor. Validity was assured through convergent validity, discriminant validity, internal consistency, and reliability. Within the structural model analysis, the GOF indices, the validity, and reliability of the factors were assessed and also the significance of the relationships (Byrne 2010).

Model Analyses and Results

In the analysis, first, the two samples were pooled into one working file to reach a model. In the CFA, two items were proved problematic and were deleted because of the correlations in two factors. However, the model with the 33 remaining items, suffered from convergent and discriminant validity issues. Hence, it was decided to assess the two samples separately.

First, in the Athens sample with the 33 items, the preliminary tests necessary for conducting SEM were carried out. That is, the assessment of normality, homoscedasticity, multicollinearity, common method bias. Having passed the preliminary tests, the EFA revealed nine reliable factors. Afterward, in the CFA, after a modification, the overall model GOF indices indicated a good fit. Convergent validity was present (the AVEs were >0.5, and composite reliabilities were >0.7). Discriminant validity was supported too (the AVEs were >0.5, and all factors' inter-scale correlations were lower than the factors' $\sqrt{AVE}$).

Table 1. Demographics

Annotation		Athens (N = 422)	Heraklion (N = 421)	Greece
Males		49.2%	48.5%	49.3%
Age	< 30	40.8%	43.2%	32.11%
	31-40	26.1%	25.3%	42%
	41-60	32.2%	32.4%	
Educational level	Below secondary education	2.1%	0.7%	29.2%
	High school education	33.9%,	27.7%	25.76%
	College degree	50.3%	51.4%	21.37%
	Masters or higher degree	13.7%	20.1%	
Use of the Internet	Beginners	3.5%	6.2%	66.6%
	Less frequent users	11%	8.1%	
	Very frequent users	85.4%	85.7%	
Internet usage	For informational purposes	88%	79.5%	
	For conducting transactions	33.6%	19.1%	
UA Index		93.33	85.07	100

Table 2. Paths, hypothesis testing, and standardized estimates for the Athenian and Heraklion samples

Path	Hypothesis	Athens Stand/zed Estimate	CR	P	Supported	Heraklion Stand/zed Estimate	C.R.	P	Supported	Supported Both samples
INT←PE	H1	.331	5.19	***	Yes	.313	3.18	.001	Yes	Yes
INT←EE	H2	.157	2.184	0.029	Yes	Ns	1.025	.306	No	No
PE←EE	H3	.666	9.944	***	Yes	.524	7.60	***	Yes	Yes
INT←SI	H4	.151	2.084	0.02	Yes	.174	2.43	.004	Yes	Yes
INT←FC	H5	.118	2.354	0.02	Yes	Ns	.191	.849	No	No
INT←HBC	H6	-.196	-4.32	***	Yes	-.250	-3.85	***	Yes	Yes
HBC←PE	H7	-.182	-2.20	0.03	Yes	-.193	-3.30	***	Yes	Yes
HBC←EE	H8	Ns	0.613	0.54	No	Ns	.279	.581	No	No
HBC←FC	H9	Ns	-1.25	0.21	No	Ns	.279	.781	No	No
INT←TOG	H10	.222	2.84	0.04	Yes	.263	4.66	***	Yes	Yes
HBC←TOG	H11	-.258	-3.02	0.003	Yes	-.275	-2.35	***	Yes	Yes
INT←TOI	H12	.273	5.04	***	Yes	.266	2.11	***	Yes	Yes
HBC←TOI	H13	-.262	-3.46	***	Yes	-.312	-5.09	***	Yes	Yes
INT←TOC	H14	Ns	0.13	0.82	No	Ns	.22	.824	No	No
HBC←TOC	H15	.315	3.78	***	Yes	.214	3.06	.002	Yes	Yes

Note: *** : p-value < 0.01.

Then after several modifications, a structural model was reached with good GOF indices. In SEM, model modification is a standard procedure that involves formulating a model based on theory and modifying it based on modification and other GOF indices (Byrne 2010). The model was modified iteratively by observing the changes in the model fit, R^2s, and the other GOF indices. AMOS printed the R^2s values for INT (the explanatory power of the model), and HBC, the standardized estimates, p-value, and critical ratio (CR) for all relationships (Table 2). There were 12 relationships (hypotheses) supported out of 15. The assessment of the Heraklion city sample was carried out next, following the same procedures and tests as with the Athens sample. After having passed the preliminary tests, the EFA results revealed nine reliable factors too. In the CFA, the model GOF indices indicated a good fit with established convergent and discriminant validity. Afterward, a structural model with an acceptable fit was reached, which was modified iteratively, to obtain the final model. Table 2 displays standardized estimates, CR, and p-value. There were 10 hypotheses supported out of 15.

The final models explained a considerable amount of variance in the data. The R^2s of the INT in the Athenian model was 0.70, while in the Heraklion was 0.65, i.e., the models explained 70% and 65% respectively of the variation in the data in predicting the intentions (Figure 2). The R^2s for the HBC were 0.22 and 0.33, respectively. In both samples, PE was the most important factor that affected INT to adopt e-government services. PE-INT was 0.33 in the Athenian sample and 0.31 in the Heraklion sample, followed by TOI-INT = 0.27 in both samples. The third strongest relation was TOG-INT (0.22, 0.26), followed by the negative HBC-INT (-0.20, -0.25) and finally by SI-INT (0.15, 0.17). The PE-EE was very strong in both samples (0.67, 0.52), meaning that PE incorporated the variance of EE. The dependent variable HBC was positively affected by TOC (0.32, 0.21), and negatively by TOI (-0.26, -0.31), TOG (-0.26, -0.28), and last PE (-0.18, -0.19). In the Athens sample only, the links EE-INT = 0.16 and FC-INT = 0.11 were significant, but still, the effects were very feeble.

The two models were configurable similar, but not necessarily metrically similar. Although, in the beginning, the assessment of the research model with the combined sample pointed for separate sample analysis, the resulting structural models showed many similarities. The variables TOI, EE, PE, INT, HBC, and SI, were represented with the same indicators in both models. Then, a model that best represented both samples' models (keeping the common paths) was drawn and depicted in Figure 2. It is nested within both samples' models, and all its paths were significant. Since the model was nested within both models, discriminant and convergent validity were present.

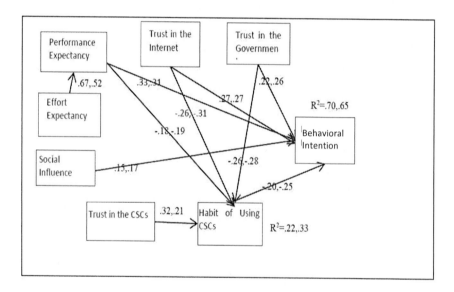

Figure 2. Research Model and Factors Influencing Adoption of e-government Services.

The multigroup moderation was carried out next, and the results revealed that gender was not a moderator to the models. Nevertheless, higher educational levels, higher ICT experience, lower age, and lower UA positively affected intention to adopt e-services. The invariance testing confirmed that for the lower age group, the explained variances of INT were higher. The R^2s of INT were also higher for the high educational and the high experienced groups than the low ones. As far as the UA is concerned, in the Athenian sample, the reading from 70% in the case of no moderation, increased to 79% for the low UA and lowered to 68% for the high UA group. In the Heraklion sample, the same estimates from 65% (no moderation) increased to 72% and decreased to 62%, respectively.

5. DISCUSSION

This research revealed the most critical factors influencing citizens' 'intention' to adopt e-government services. In both models, 'performance expectancy' exhibited the strongest effect on 'intention' to use e-services. As e-services offer a quicker service method and practical benefits, then 'performance expectancy' of a user rises, and also the 'intention' to use e-services. 'Performance expectancy' was revealed as the most influential determinant of INT in other models, too, e.g., TAM, TPB, UTAUT, and UTAUT2. The 'effort expectancy' affected 'performance expectancy' directly, meaning that the latter incorporated variance from 'effort expectancy'. It was in line with other studies using the UTAUT or UTAUT2 models (Slade et al. 2015; Gao and Deng 2012). The 'effort expectancy' did not affect 'intention' to use directly. The same results were obtained in other studies using the UTAUT2 and in e-government settings (Krishnaraju, Mathew and Sugumaran 2013; Vinodh and Mathew 2016). Usually, the 'effort expectancy' affects intention directly when the website interface or the technology used is complicated, and individuals are less experienced (Venkatesh et al. 2003; Taylor and Todd 1995), which did not apply in this case. Hence, hypotheses H1 and H3 were supported, while H2 was not.

The Trust factors (TOG and TOI) comprised the second and third strongest determinants in both models. Despite that, most probably, they were more critical than 'performance expectancy.' They have been acknowledged to affect the willingness to use e-government services (Belanger and Carter 2008; Carter and Weerakkody 2008; Fakhoury and Baker 2016). When there is a lack of trust in the Internet or the e-service provider, citizens will be less likely to utilize e-government services or change their habits of going to CSCs. The significant adverse relationship between the trust factors (TOI, TOG) and 'habit of going to the CSCs' confirmed the argument. Hence, hypotheses H10, H11, H12, and H13 were supported.

The 'habit of going to CSCs' was negatively related to 'intention' to use. Then, H6 was supported. Peoples' established habit of getting serviced in the CSCs, decreased their intentions to use e-services. Venkatesh et al. (2012) found that the habit-INT effect of being very significant and positive, and the difference with the findings of this study was due to the type of 'habit' being examined.

Both samples showed a weak relationship between SI and INT. Most probably, the substantial impact of the trust factors (TOI, TOG) on 'intention' lessened the strength of the relationships (Sun and Zhang 2006). In this study, Athens and Heraklion city residents did not rely much on significant others to be convinced to use municipal e-services because they were more concerned about the trust issues. The path FC-INT was insignificant, being in-line with other e-government studies using the UTAUT2 model (Moraes and Meirelles 2016; Vinodh and Mathew 2013; Krishnaraju, Mathew and Sugumaran 2016).

For both samples, the link 'trust in the CSCs' – 'habit of going to CSCs' was positive and significant, meaning that people go to CSCs because they trust them. Besides that, the adverse effects of PE, TOG, TOI on HBC made the point that the lack of 'performance expectancy' (benefits gained) and lack of trust drove people to get serviced in the CSCs. 'Trust in the CSCs' did not affect 'intention' to use e-services. On the contrary, a feeble negative indirect effect through the 'habit of using CSCs' was present. The established trust in the CSCs affected negatively the intention to use e-services. The argument that citizens' interaction and transaction with government online via a trusted third party enhances trust in e-government services and increases e-government usage (Al-Sobhi 2011) did not apply.

The relationships between EE-HBC and FC-HBC were insignificant. Hence hypotheses H4, H7, and H15 were supported, while H5, H8, H9, and H14 were not.

The results also suggested that the impacts on the dependent variables differed with age, education, experience, and UA, but not gender. There was no difference between males and females in the 'intention' to use e-services. The other demographics strengthened or decreased the power of the dependent variables on INT and HBC. The UA variable, in particular, was revealed as the most potent moderator as it strongly affected INT and HBC, in both models. Based on the findings presented above, the hypothesis 16 was not supported, while the hypotheses H17, H18m, H19, and H20 were partially supported. The significance of the moderating effects in the models suggested that different groups of residents attached different weights to various factors that influenced their intentions to use technology. Younger persons, more educated, savvy in using technology, or those with low UA seemed to be the early adopters. On the contrary, older adults, people with low education, low internet literate, or high in UA were less willing to adopt e-government services and preferred to communicate with their government via the CSCs. Thus, when the goal is to facilitate 'shifts' in citizens' habitual intention, as in this case, more resources may need to be targeted to these groups.

By extending the UTAUT2 model and testing it for the impact of the trust dimensions on the INT and HBC variables, it provided theoretical and practical support of the very significant role of the trust factors in the intention to use e-services and in the e-government adoption in Greece. Also, the fact that the 'habit of going to CSCs' and 'trust in the CSCs' factors have never been previously proposed presented an opportunity for theoretical and practical implications. The relationships concerning 'habit of going to CSCs' that were found are of particular interest, although they were mainly based on the data, as literature for intermediaries is emerging (Al-Shobhi 2011). This study also revealed the primary drivers of citizens going to CSCs; hence, it is possible to provide fruitful recommendations to policymakers.

6. IMPLICATIONS FOR POLICYMAKERS

This research has practical implications for practitioners, policymakers, and web designers on how e-citizens might increase their willingness to interact online. Government agencies should consider actions, policy measures and marketing strategies to 'shift' citizens' behavior to the electronic channel ('Channel shift') (Mundy, Umer, and Foster 2011). First, 'performance expectancy' and 'effort expectancy' are crucial determinants of e-government acceptance and should be increased. As e-services provide benefits, i.e., convenient access, prompt service, efficiency, and effectiveness in conjunction with traditional services, then the 'perceived performance' of a user rises, and the intention to use e-services increases. It is also vital for government agencies to provide usable, useful, up-to-date, accurate, and reliable information and services via their websites to increase 'perceived performance'. Nielsen and Loranger (2006) give a list of the features that make a website usable. An intuitive interface is a must, but search and support facilities, online help, telephone helplines, and documentation should be available on the website and alongside the e-services. A transformation to more open and user-friendly e-government is needed. Researchers insist that usability is critical because it enhances trust in the user, which in turn increases adoption (Bedi and Banati 2006). In Greece, the online help is not available on most of the government websites, and the central government helpline '1500' has ceased its operation (Voutinioti 2014b). Specifically, the telephone helpline should restart its operation for delivering information and assistance to the people by phone. Next, by offering transactional services, users finalize their services electronically, and the usefulness of e-services is increased (Carter and Weerakkody 2008). For conducting government transactions, thought, e-identification and e-signature are vital. In Greece, e-identification has been issued to selected government employees (head of divisions) only.

Users' trust should be enhanced. The Internet should be a reliable technology, and there should have taken the necessary security measures and performance structures of this electronic medium. The Greek government should make e-services and the Internet more trustworthy by improving the legal infrastructure (laws for privacy, e-signature, and knowledge acquisition law). The government agencies should secure the data and establish a safer environment for citizen transactions; citizens should be aware of the security measures used (Voutinioti 2013; Al-Sobhi 2011). Trust in the government agency, depending on the image of the organization providing the e-service, has to be enhanced. Influencing this type of trust is a long-term effort. In the long run, government institutions should increase their reputation by establishing consistent government policies, looking after citizens' needs, being open and transparent, fighting corruption, and increasing the field of civil rights. In the short run, marketing tools should be used to increase the awareness of the provision of e-services, the benefits gained, and the utilization of the security mechanisms. For increasing awareness, campaigns should be designed to communicate utilitarian messages effectively, through product brochures, newspapers, CD-ROMs, radio, TV, and by using e-government 2.0 tools (e.g., social media, forums). The campaigns should follow the 'market segmentation strategy', by targeting the younger, more educated, more ICT experienced and innovative, because these groups seem to be the early adopters.

Citizens' 'habit of going to the CSCs' affected 'intention' negatively, and as the main drivers were revealed, the lack of 'trust' and 'performance expectancy'. Hence, the above-proposed strategies will lessen this antagonistic relationship. 'Trust in the CSCs' drove people to go to the CSCs' to get serviced because they trusted them. On the contrary, 'trust in the CSCs' did not drive people to use e-services, meaning that CSCs did not play a key role in increasing e-government take-up. The explanation most probably lies in the way CSCs operate, i.e., mostly inform about government issues and conduct the services on citizens' behalf. Hence, it is proposed that these trusted entities (CSCs) have to be dynamic and re-establish their roles in the new electronic environment (re-intermediation) (Al-Sobhi 2011). In the marketing strategies, CSCs should play a vital role, by informing citizens about the practical implications and benefits gained and also guide them in self-using the e-services. As CSCs' employees are well ICT trained and users of government portals, they should provide the necessary training in using e-services on the spot. For example, by using 'market segmentation' strategies (i.e., targeting the younger, innovative), they should inform clients waiting in line to get serviced, about the availability of e-services and assist them in their usage, by any medium available, i.e., computers, laptops, PDAs, citizens' smartphones. Then a valid promotion and use of e-services and the 'channel shifting' process will be achieved. This model is scalable and will lead to the gradual shift of citizens' behavior to the electronic medium.

This chapter investigated the most important factors affecting the intention to use the e-services and developed and validated an e-government adoption model based on the theory of UTAUT2. The results of the analyses proved that the predictor variables of the UTAUT2, in addition to the trust factors, actually predicted the e-government adoption behavior well. It also emphasized the essential channels the CSCs and indicated that if the government works closely with CSCs and 're-intermediate', e-government usage will increase in Greece.

REFERENCES

Ajzen, Icek. (1991). "The Theory of Planned Behaviour." *Organizational Behaviour and Human Decision Processes*, Vol *50*, No 2, 179-211.

Al-Hujran, O., Al-Dalahmeh, M. & Aloudat, A. (2011). "The Role of National Culture on Citizen Adoption of E-Government Services: An Empirical Study." *Electronic Journal of E-government*, *9*(2), 93 – 106.

Al-Sebie, Madi. (2014). "Organizational Challenges Facing Integrating E-Government Systems: An Empirical Study". *European Scientific Journal*, No 10, Vol *10*, 236–250.

Al-Sobhi, Faris. (2011). *The Roles of Intermediaries in the Adoption of E-Government Services in Saudi Arabia*. PhD diss., Brunel University, UK.

Alexa. (2017). *Amazon's company that accounts for traffic in the websites.* Accessed January 2018. http://www.alexa.com.

Bedi, Punam. & Banati, Hema. (2006). "Assessing User Trust to Improve Web Usability". *Journal of Computer Science*, Vol *2*, No 3, 283-287.

Belanger, France. & Carter, Lemuria. (2008). "Trust and risk in e-government adoption." *The Journal of Strategic Information Systems*, Vol *17*, No 2, 165-176.

Byrne, Barbara. M. (2010). *Structural equation modeling with AMOS: Basic concepts, applications, and programming* (2nd ed.). New York, NY: Taylor & Francis Group.

Cabinakova, Johana., Kroenung, Julia., Eckhardt, Andreas. & Bernius, Steffen. (2013). The importance of culture, trust, and habitual patterns - determinants of cross-cultural e-government adoption. In the *21st European Conference on Information Systems*. The Netherlands. Utrecht June 6-8.

Carter, Lemuria. & Belanger, France. (2005). "The utilization of e-Government services: Citizen trust, innovation, and acceptance factors." *Information Systems Journal*, Vol *15*, No 1, 5–25.

Carter, Lemuria. & Weerakkody, Vishanth. (2008). "E-government adoption: A cultural comparison." *Information Systems Frontiers*, Vol *10*, No 4, 473-482.

Davis, Fred. D. (1989). "Perceived usefulness, perceived ease of use, and user acceptance of information technology." *MIS Quarterly*, Vol *13*, No 3, 319-340.

Eurobarometer. (2018). *Standard Eurobarometer 90*. European Commission. Accessed June 19. https://ec.europa.eu/commfrontoffice/ publicopinion/index.cfm/survey/getsurveydetail/instruments/standard/s urveyky/2215.

European Commission, *Digital Economy and Society Index (DESI)*. (2018). Accessed June 19. https://ec.europa.eu/digital-single-market/ en/european-digital-progress-report.

Fakhoury, Rania. & Baker, David. (2016). "Governmental Trust, Active Citizenship, and E-Government Acceptance in Lebanon." *Journal of Leadership, Accountability and Ethics*, Vol *13*, No 2, 36.

Fan, Qiuyan. (2015). "E-government development at the local level in Australia using a framework for connected e-government." In

Encyclopedia of Information Science and Technology, 2719-2725, 3rd ed. New York: IGI-Global.

Gao, Ting Ting. & Deng, Yanhong. (2012). A study on users' acceptance behavior to mobile e-books application based on the UTAUT model. *3rd International Conference on Software Engineering and Service Science, ICSESS - Proc. IEEE*, 376-379.

Gefen, David. Warkentin, Merrill. Pavlou, Paul. & Rose, Gregory. (2002). "E-government adoption". *Americas Conference on Information Systems*, 569-576, Dallas, TX, August.

Hofstede, Geert. (2011). Dimensionalizing Cultures: The Hofstede Model in Context. *Online Readings in Psychology and Culture*, 2(1). http://dx.doi.org/10.9707/2307-0919.1014. Accessed: 10 January.

ITRE (The European Parliament's Industry Research and Energy Committee). (2014). *Report Mapping Smart Cities in the EU*. Available at: http://www.europarl.europa.eu/RegData/ etudes/etudes/join/2014/507480/IPOLITRE_ET(2014)507480_EN.pdf. (Accessed: 10 May 2015).

'Kallikratis'. (2011). *The local government reform program.* Accessed July 19. http://kallikratis.ypes.gr/.

Krishnaraju, Vinodh K., Mathew, Saji. & Sugumaran, Vijayan. (2016). "Web personalization for user acceptance of technology: An empirical investigation of E-government services." *Information Systems Frontiers*, *18*, 579-595.

Moraes, Gustavo Hermínio Salati Marcondes. & Meirelles, Fernando de Souza. (2016). "User's perspective of Electronic Government adoption in Brazil." *Journal of Technology Management and Innovation*, Vol *11*, No 3, 122-144. ·

Mundy, Darren. Umer, Qasim. & Foster, Alastair. (2011). "Examining the Potential for Channel Shift in the UK through Multiple Lenses." *Electronic Journal of e-Government*, Vol *9*, No 2, 203-213.

Nielsen, Jakob. & Loranger, Hoa. (2006). *Prioritizing Web usability* (6th ed.). Berkeley, CA: New Riders.

Rana, Nripendra. Dwivedi, Yogesh. & Williams, Michael. (2013). "Evaluating alternative theoretical models for examining citizen-centric adoption of e-government". *Transforming Government: People, Process and Policy*, Vol 7, No 1, 27-49.

Rogers, Everett. (2003). Diffusion of innovations. New York, NY: The Free Press.

Sarikas, Omiros. & Weerakkody, Vishanth. (2007). "Realising integrated e-government services: a UK local government perspective." *Transforming Government, People, Process and Policy*, Vol 1, No 2, 153-173.

Slade, Emma. Williams, Michael., Dwivedi, Yogesh. & Piercy, Niall. (2015). "Exploring consumer adoption of proximity mobile payments." *Journal of Strategic Marketing*, Vol 23, No 3, 209-223.

Sun, Heshan. & Zhang, Ping. (2006). "The role of moderating factors in user technology acceptance." *International Journal of Human-Computer Studies*, Vol 64, No 2, 53-78.

Susanto, Tony Dwi. & Goodwin, Robert. (2013). "User Acceptance of SMS-based e-Government Services: Differences between Adopters and Non-Adopters." *Government Information Quarterly*, Vol 30, No 4, 486-497.

Taylor, Shirley. & Todd, Peter. (1995). "Decomposition and crossover effects in the theory of planned behavior: A study of consumer adoption intentions. *International Journal of Research in Marketing*, No 12, vol 2, 137-155.

Venkatesh, Viswanath. Morris, Michael. Davis, Gordon. & Davis, Fred. (2003). "User acceptance of information technology: toward a unified view." *MIS Quarterly*, Vol 27, No 3, 425-478.

Venkatesh, Viswanath. Thong, James. & Xin, Xu. (2012). "Consumer Acceptance and Use of Information Technology: Extending the Unified Theory." *MIS Quarterly*, Vol 36, No 1, 157–78.

Vinodh, Krishnaraju. & Mathew, Saji. K. (2013). "Web personalization research – An Information Systems perspective." *Journal of Systems and Information Technology*, Vol 15, No 3, 254-268.

Voutinioti, Anastasia. (2013). "Determinants of User Adoption of e-Government Services in Greece and the Role of Citizen Service Centres." *Procedia Technology*, 8, 238–244.

Voutinioti, Anastasia. (2014a). "Determinants of user adoption of e-government services: the case of Greek Local Government." *International Journal of Technology Marketing,* Vol 9, No 3, 234 - 251.

Voutinioti, Anastasia. (2014b). "The roles of Citizen Service Centres in e-government adoption in Greece." *7th Annual Conference of the EuroMed Academy of Business*, 1698-1709. Norway, Kristiansand, September 18-19.

INDEX

A

accenture, 98, 134
access, 20, 23, 24, 25, 45, 78, 107, 112, 123, 139, 147, 156
age, 7, 128, 141, 144, 152, 155
agencies, 4, 6, 9, 10, 13, 14, 15, 17, 18, 19, 20, 21, 24, 27, 28, 29, 30, 68, 78, 107, 110, 111, 113, 114, 115, 116, 117, 118, 129, 139, 142, 143, 147, 156, 157

B

barriers, xi, 18, 45, 61, 137, 141, 143
benefits, 43, 45, 99, 115, 138, 142, 153, 154, 156, 157
Blue House business process management system (BH-BPS), 128
BPR (Business Process Reengineering), 92, 108, 123, 126, 129
BPR/ISP, 108, 129
Britain, 31
broadband, 8, 14, 15, 16
budget allocation, 134
business management, 124
business processes, 45, 58, 101, 112, 115, 120, 129
Business Reference Model (BRM), 33, 108, 111, 112
Business Support Services (G4B), 109, 114
businesses, 9, 10, 15, 17, 18, 20, 22, 23, 24, 28, 68, 101, 104, 114, 116, 117

C

challenges, vii, ix, 34, 37, 42
changing environment, 110
cities, 84, 146, 147
citizen service centers, viii, xi, 137, 138
citizens, viii, xi, 4, 9, 10, 13, 15, 20, 22, 23, 24, 26, 28, 41, 42, 44, 104, 111, 112, 114, 117, 137, 138, 139, 140, 142, 143, 144, 146, 147, 153, 154, 155, 156, 157
citizenship, 43, 45, 61
civil rights, 157
civil servants, 72, 104
civil service, 102, 103, 107, 111, 112
Clinton, President, 95

communication, 9, 12, 13, 14, 37, 91, 101, 117
communication technologies, 91
community, viii, 42, 52, 64, 124
computer, 7, 14, 18, 19, 20, 22, 23, 25, 31, 37, 114
computer systems, 23
conference, 21, 31, 46, 53, 131
construction, 91, 103, 111, 113, 123
cooperation, 26, 101, 103, 116, 120, 122, 124
coordination, 121, 122, 123
correlations, 148, 149
corruption, 35, 120, 124, 157
cost, 10, 16, 115, 117, 142
cultural norms, 6
culture, 92, 124, 159

D

data analysis, 18
data processing, 2, 17, 18, 19, 20
data rates, 14
data set, 17
database, 33
decentralization, 121
decision-making process, 18, 94
Deloitte, 97, 135
democracy, 5, 44, 96, 97, 102, 106
demographic data, 147
demonstrations, 10
Denmark, x, 1, 14, 16, 28, 39, 56, 89, 91
dependent variable, 151, 155
deregulation, 30
designers, xi, 138, 156
developed countries, 20
developing countries, 116
diffusion, x, 10, 90, 139
digital democracy, 5, 96, 97
diplomacy, 10, 11, 13, 111
direct investment, 117

E

e-commerce, 26
economic crisis, 102
economic development, 24
economic growth, 26, 90
education, 118, 128, 149, 155
e-government, v, vi, vii, viii, ix, x, xi, 1, 2, 3, 4, 6, 8, 11, 12, 15, 16, 18, 19, 20, 22, 23, 24, 25, 26, 27, 28, 29, 30, 33, 34, 35, 36, 37, 38, 39, 41, 42, 43, 44, 45, 47, 48, 49, 51, 52, 53, 54, 56, 57, 58, 59, 60, 61, 63, 64, 67, 68, 69, 70, 71, 72, 73,74, 77, 78, 79, 81, 82, 83, 84, 85, 86, 89, 90, 91, 92, 93, 94, 95, 96, 97, 98, 99, 100, 101, 102, 103, 104, 105, 106, 107, 108, 109, 114, 115, 116, 117, 118, 119, 120, 121, 122, 124, 125, 126, 127, 128, 130, 131, 132, 133, 134, 135, 136, 137, 138, 139, 140, 142, 143, 144, 146, 147, 151, 152, 153, 154, 155, 156, 157, 158, 159, 160, 161, 162
E-Government Act, 103, 135
e-government adoption, viii, xi, 137, 138, 139, 141, 144, 155, 158, 159, 160, 162
e-government day, 131
E-government Development Index, 91
e-government leadership, 99, 119, 125
e-Government Roadmap, x, 89, 106, 107, 108, 121
Electronic Government, 35, 42, 61, 63, 64, 83, 94, 135, 136, 160
empirical methods, 69
employees, 16, 23, 44, 99, 143, 147, 156, 157
employment, 78, 114, 116
enforcement, 118, 124
engineering, 62, 63, 64
enterprise architecture, v, vii, ix, 41, 42, 43, 44, 45, 47, 48, 49, 52, 54, 56, 60, 61, 62, 63, 65

environment, 83, 102, 107, 111, 118, 143, 157
environments, 143
e-participation Index, 91
Europe, 7, 9, 10, 11, 12, 13, 15, 18, 19, 20, 22, 23, 28, 32, 56, 58, 60, 62, 63, 147
European Commission, 140, 159
European Parliament, 160
European Union, 23, 26, 31
evaluation, v, vii, ix, 61, 67, 68, 69, 70, 71, 72, 73, 76, 77, 79, 81, 82, 83, 84, 85, 86, 120, 123, 129, 130, 131, 132, 133
evidence, 2, 3, 7, 8, 13, 15, 19, 46
evolution, viii, ix, 12, 13, 14, 18, 19, 20, 21, 22, 30, 42, 63

F

factor analysis, 148
federal government, 38, 94, 95
financial, 91, 102, 111, 143
financial crisis, 102
financial institutions, 111
food safety, 114
force, 28, 103, 105, 120
foreign exchange, 115
framework, ix, xi, 5, 6, 29, 30, 35, 42, 43, 46, 48, 49, 54, 55, 56, 59, 60, 61, 64, 65, 84, 86, 93, 98, 101, 112, 136, 137, 159
Framework Act on Informatization Promotion, 93

G

Gore, Vice President Al, 96, 133
governance, 4, 44, 46, 95, 119, 124, 134, 138
government budget, 126
government business process management system (On-Nara BPS), 128, 129
Government for Citizen (G4C), 104, 112

government policy, xi, 121, 131, 133, 138
government services, vii, viii, x, 1, 2, 3, 4, 5, 6, 7, 8, 9, 10, 11, 12, 13, 14, 15, 16, 18, 19, 20, 21, 22, 23, 24, 25, 26, 27, 28, 29, 30, 39, 61, 64, 68, 70, 84, 103, 104, 107, 117, 138, 140, 142, 143, 151, 153, 154, 155, 159, 161, 162
governments, viii, ix, 11, 15, 16, 21, 22, 23, 28, 30, 41, 51, 59, 67, 68, 98, 111, 117, 138
Greece, vi, viii, x, xi, 56, 67, 68, 69, 70, 77, 78, 82, 137, 138, 139, 140, 146, 149, 155, 156, 158, 161, 162
guiding principles, 98

H

harmonization, 25
health, 17
health information, 17
higher education, 152
history, 7, 8, 25, 32, 33, 34, 35, 36, 37, 39, 91, 100, 124
Home Tax Service, 104, 113
human, 12, 57, 61, 91, 104, 107, 111, 116
human resources, 58, 61, 104, 107, 111
hypothesis, 150, 155
hypothesis test, 150

I

ideal, 76, 77, 79, 80, 81, 82
identification, 4, 48, 111, 139, 156
immigration, 23, 115
impeachment, 128
improvements, 62
information exchange, 5, 10, 12, 13
information sharing, 111, 116
information technology, 16, 68, 95, 96, 100, 103, 119, 131, 159, 161

infrastructure, 45, 63, 91, 102, 103, 108, 123, 124, 125, 126, 141, 157
institution, 2, 5, 6, 7, 9, 10, 11, 13, 16, 17, 22, 26, 27, 30, 33, 110, 129, 143
institutional change, 30
institutional theory, 2
institutions, vii, viii, 1, 2, 3, 4, 5, 6, 8, 10, 11, 13, 14, 15, 16, 18, 19, 20, 21, 22, 23, 24, 25, 27, 28, 29, 30, 58, 62, 92, 93, 101, 102, 110, 118, 124, 157
interface, 78, 83, 153, 156
intermediaries, xi, 137, 143, 155
internal consistency, 148
internal processes, viii, 41
international standards, 108
interoperability, ix, 26, 29, 42, 43, 107
investments, ix, 45, 67, 68, 116, 127
issues, ix, 21, 32, 67, 68, 95, 102, 117, 139, 140, 149, 154, 157

K

knowledge acquisition, 157
Korea, vii, x, xi, 33, 89, 90, 91, 92, 93, 99, 100, 101, 104, 105, 106, 113, 116, 118, 120, 121, 126, 127, 128, 129, 130, 131, 132, 133, 134, 135, 136

L

labor markets, 114
landscapes, 106
languages, 48, 49, 78
laws, 5, 20, 24, 93, 101, 103, 112, 118, 157
laws and regulations, 118
leadership, x, 90, 91, 92, 93, 95, 97, 98, 99, 105, 119, 125, 131, 133
learning, 21, 85, 125, 128, 142
legislation, 20, 35, 118, 139

local government, viii, 35, 37, 41, 42, 43, 49, 61, 64, 104, 108, 111, 113, 129, 138, 139, 140, 142, 143, 147, 160, 161, 162
local government reform, 160
logistic services, 115
logistics, 115

M

management, vii, viii, x, 6, 10, 11, 17, 20, 24, 33, 42, 43, 44, 64, 90, 97, 103, 110, 111, 112, 113, 115, 117, 119, 121, 122, 123, 125, 128, 129, 135
mapping, vii, ix, 31, 42, 64
market segment, 157, 158
marketing, 115, 156, 157
messages, 9, 11, 20, 157
methodology, 43, 46, 61, 139
models, 45, 139, 140, 141, 143, 146, 151, 152, 153, 155, 160
moderating factors, 161
modifications, 20, 151
momentum, 121, 132
motivation, 142
multimedia, 12, 14
multimedia services, 12
municipal e-government, 42
municipality, ix, 42, 43, 49, 58, 61, 147

N

National CIO, 133
National Computing & Information Administration (NCIA), 116, 118
national culture, 142
national emergency, 112
National Information Society Agency (NIA), 121

Index

O

officials, 17, 93, 95, 97, 120, 121, 124, 129, 143, 147
operations, 110
opportunities, vii, ix, 20, 42, 98
overseas investment, 115

P

participants, viii, 41, 71, 147
participatory democracy, 106, 122
personal computers, 8
policy, x, 2, 21, 25, 29, 33, 90, 91, 92, 93, 103, 105, 106, 111, 116, 123, 124, 125, 131, 132, 133, 134, 156
policymakers, 139, 155, 156
political leaders, 91, 98
political system, 91
politics, 33, 110, 128
population, 13, 147, 148
portfolio, viii, 1, 2
postal service, 9, 11, 13, 14, 32
predictor variables, 158
preparation, iv, 101, 112
presidency, 119, 120, 122, 127
Presidential Committee on Government Innovation and Decentralization (PCGID), 105, 118, 121, 122, 123, 125, 136
principles, ix, 42, 45, 99, 103
private sector, 12, 17, 123
project, vii, viii, 1, 2, 91, 93, 102, 105, 108, 111, 112, 114, 115, 116, 117, 118, 119, 121, 124, 126, 129, 134
public administration, 106, 116
public officials, 120, 124, 125
public sector, 61, 63, 95, 120
public service, ix, 2, 4, 16, 44, 68, 69, 106, 114, 124, 140
public services, ix, 2, 4, 31, 44, 68, 69, 140

Q

quality of life, 45
quality of service, 15
quantitative research, xi, 137
questionnaire, 138, 144, 146, 147

R

recommendations, iv, xi, 138, 155
reform, 95, 120, 121, 123, 131, 139
regulations, 5, 10, 118, 124, 143
resource management, 118
resources, 24, 26, 98, 99, 103, 107, 116, 138, 139, 143, 155
rules, 5, 14, 17, 26, 30

S

search terms, 48, 49
secondary education, 149
security, 82, 95, 107, 139, 156
service provider, 143, 153
services, iv, vii, viii, ix, x, 1, 2, 3, 4, 5, 6, 7, 8, 9, 10, 11, 12, 13, 14, 15, 16, 18, 19, 20, 21, 22, 23, 24, 25, 26, 27, 28, 29, 30, 41, 42, 43, 44, 45, 61, 62, 68, 70, 78, 80, 82, 84, 103, 104, 107, 108, 111, 112, 113, 114, 115, 117, 123, 131, 138, 139, 140, 142, 143, 144, 146, 151, 152, 153, 154, 155, 156, 157, 158, 159, 160, 161, 162
society, 5, 9, 12, 13, 17, 30, 116, 124, 140
software, 21, 46, 62, 63, 64, 69, 73, 84, 85, 119
South Asian Association for Regional Cooperation, 26
South Korea, v, x, 23, 28, 56, 89, 90, 91, 92, 93, 100, 120, 127, 128, 129, 130
structure, 45, 71, 101, 118

success factors of e-government, 92, 96
systematic literature mapping, v, vii, ix, 41, 42, 43, 46, 60
Systematic Literature Mapping, v, 41, 43, 46, 60

T

technological advancement, 91
technology, vii, viii, ix, 1, 2, 3, 4, 6, 7, 8, 9, 10, 11, 13, 14, 15, 16, 17, 18, 19, 20, 21, 22, 23, 24, 25, 26, 27, 28, 29, 30, 32, 33, 34, 35, 36, 38, 39, 42, 43, 46, 55, 58, 63, 64, 68, 73, 75, 84, 85, 86, 87, 93, 94, 95, 96, 97, 100, 103, 109, 119, 131, 134, 136, 141, 153, 155, 156, 159, 160, 161, 162
telecommunications, 126
telephone, 12, 13, 14, 23, 32, 36, 156
Time Lag Effect, 132
transactions, 28, 139, 146, 148, 149, 156, 157
transformation, 45, 134, 156
transparency, 45, 102, 106, 120, 123, 129

U

UN e-Government Survey, x, 89, 91, 135, 136
United Kingdom, 37, 56, 97
United Nations, 24, 27, 33, 38, 86, 91, 132, 136
United States, 13, 16, 32, 33, 38, 58, 63, 94, 95, 96, 97, 135
UTAUT2, xi, 137, 138, 139, 140, 141, 142, 144, 153, 154, 155, 158

V

validation, xi, 73, 75, 137
valuation, 68, 120, 130, 132
variables, 141, 142, 144, 152, 155
vision, 21, 27, 91, 95, 96, 98, 99, 102, 103, 105, 106, 107, 123, 130, 132

W

web, xi, 4, 20, 33, 44, 63, 78, 112, 138, 139, 142, 156
web service, 142
websites, ix, 7, 67, 68, 69, 70, 71, 72, 73, 74, 76, 77, 79, 80, 81, 82, 83, 84, 140, 142, 147, 156, 158
workforce, 58, 61, 118